Classroom as Organization

TEACHING METHODS IN BUSINESS

Series Editors: Jeanie M. Forray, *Western New England University, USA*, Jennifer S.A. Leigh, *Nazareth College, USA* and Sarah L. Wright, *University of Canterbury, New Zealand*

Contemporary business education encompasses a wide range of disciplines with all business faculty expected to teach effectively. Yet, in establishing that expectation, business schools don't always consider what resources educators may need to become effective teachers or to continue to develop their craft. The Teaching Methods in Business (TMB) series is designed to address that gap.

Every TMB volume provides focused, informative, and immediately useful coverage of a single active learning method with relevant considerations for any type of business classroom. Authored by interdisciplinary teams of business educators, the series has been planned and edited for a global audience.

Each TMB volume begins with a discussion of a specific teaching method within its theoretical and historical roots. Following this foundation, each volume discusses how the method meets the needs of particular learners in specific ways, offers reflection on the method's strengths and challenges, and provides examples of how the method may be implemented in various contexts. All volumes conclude with a list of annotated references drawn from pedagogical journals in business and related resources. The series is tailored for business educators at all levels of experience, from doctoral students in their first teaching assignment to experienced full-time faculty looking to refresh or expand their teaching repertoire. The series is also intended as a resource for adjunct instructors, libraries and university teaching centers.

The TMB series takes both a scholarly and an applied approach to educator development by providing conceptual grounding along with practical guidance and resources needed to implement the method based on the specific needs of the reader. Regardless of your particular business discipline or your experience with engaged learning, we hope you find the information provided in this and other volumes both inspiring and useful!

Titles in the series include:

Classroom as Organization
Debby R. Thomas, Stacie F. Chappell with David S. Bright

Role-Play Simulations
Alexander R. Bolinger and Julie V. Stanton

Forthcoming titles include:

Experiential Exercises in the Classroom
Mary K. Foster, Vicki Taylor and Jennie Walker

Project and Problem Based Learning
Gary Coombs and Janelle E. Goodnight

Computer Simulations and Gaming
James W. Cooper, Michele E. Yoder and Stacey L. Watson

Group and Team Work
Ricardo Flores and Antonina Bauman

Course Design and Learning Assessment
Kathy Lund Dean, Nancy S. Niemi and Charles J. Fornaciari

Classroom as Organization

Debby R. Thomas

Assistant Professor of Management, College of Business, George Fox University, USA

Stacie F. Chappell

Associate Dean, Graduate Programs, Faculty of Management, Vancouver Island University, Canada

with

David S. Bright

Professor and Department Chair, Raj Soin College of Business, Wright State University, USA

TEACHING METHODS IN BUSINESS

 Edward Elgar
PUBLISHING

Cheltenham, UK • Northampton, MA, USA

Published by
Edward Elgar Publishing Limited
The Lypiatts
15 Lansdown Road
Cheltenham
Glos GL50 2JA
UK

Edward Elgar Publishing, Inc.
William Pratt House
9 Dewey Court
Northampton
Massachusetts 01060
USA

A catalogue record for this book
is available from the British Library

Library of Congress Control Number: 2020940507

This book is available electronically in the **Elgar**online
Business subject collection
http://dx.doi.org/10.4337/9781788979856

Printed on elemental chlorine free (ECF)
recycled paper containing 30% Post-Consumer Waste

ISBN 978 1 78897 984 9 (cased)
ISBN 978 1 78897 986 3 (paperback)
ISBN 978 1 78897 985 6 (eBook)

Printed and bound in the USA

This book is dedicated to Roger Putzel, Emeritus Professor at Saint Michael's College in Colchester, Vermont. Roger is the common thread in all of our stories; his passion for Classroom as Organization (CAO) is infectious, and it is this spirit that has been most influential in our work. It is fair to say that without his vision and tireless mentoring, none of us would have embraced CAO or fully understood its potential as a powerful, transformational teaching and learning approach.

Contents

Figures

1. Introduction to *Classroom as Organization*

In this book, the authors describe the Classroom as Organization (CAO) teaching method, a highly experiential approach to classroom structure and management. They provide readers with information about the background of the method, considerations for its use, implementation ideas and resources for additional reading.

Chapter 2 begins with an overview of the historical context in which CAO emerged, and the teaching philosophy of educational constructivism that provides the theoretical basis for core teaching strategies in CAO. In addition, the chapter includes a synthesis of the CAO literature: identifying seminal articles, tracing the expansion of the methodology, and identifying themes specific to the CAO framework. Recognizing the diversity of both published and unpublished CAO designs, the authors conclude the chapter with a discussion of common CAO elements, including interdependence, peer assessment, student learning and management roles, instructor delegation as a senior manager, and the balance of structure and ambiguity to support learning.

In Chapter 3, the authors introduce key considerations for using CAO by describing the inner workings of the CAO methodology and assessing its utility for a given course. The chapter focuses on two sets of key considerations when contemplating the use of CAO. The first considerations address whether CAO is a good fit with the educator's teaching philosophy, the institutional context, the basic parameters of the course, and the cognitive and affective learning objectives. The second set of considerations relate to design elements specific to the CAO approach, including organizational design, team descriptions, peer teaching, peer assessment, assessment structures, and end-of-semester evaluation. For advanced experiential learning instructors, the authors discuss considerations for tailoring CAO instructional designs.

Chapter 4 contains a complete CAO course design for an upper-level organizational behavior course, OB Inc., explained in the context of the considerations discussed in Chapter 3. A set of appendices are provided that enable educators to adopt and adapt the design.

In Chapter 5, the authors provide an annotated bibliography of forty seminal articles in the CAO literature. While CAO sits within the broader domain of experience-based learning, the articles included in the bibliography focus directly on CAO. The bibliography is structured in chronological order so the reader can see the earliest approaches to CAO design along with later adaptations to entrepreneurship, leadership, and introduction to business courses.

2. Conceptual and theoretical frame

Sam had just finished teaching a class and was feeling discouraged. Her students seemed disengaged, sleepy, and uninterested. Their participation in the discussion was lackluster. They appeared eager to leave class and get on with their day. She felt unsure whether her teaching was connecting with the students: Did they get it? Were they really learning something useful? Did her teaching matter? For what seemed like the millionth time, Sam wondered aloud how she might build more engagement while making the course more practical and impactful for students.

As Sam returned to her office, she heard a commotion coming from Maria's classroom. She paused at the classroom door to see what was happening. Her mouth fell open in surprise. Students were talking, interacting, and moving around the room. They seemed 100 percent engrossed. Sam assumed that Maria was leading an activity, but she had to look around the room to find Maria observing the class from the back. The students were leading the class on their own. This classroom did not look like any Sam had ever seen before; in fact, it looked more like a typical workplace environment with multiple teams engaged in projects. What could Maria be doing to make her classroom function that way? Sam made a mental note to talk to Maria to learn more.

1. INTRODUCTION

Sam's conundrum is all too familiar: Educators want to create an engaging classroom environment where students are committed to their learning. And yet, many struggle in knowing exactly how to create that kind of environment. On the one hand, there is pressure to cover a defined set of concepts. On the other, it is important that students internalize and apply what they are learning. Given the inherent tension between covering content and student engagement (Hung et al., 2003), how do educators best serve students in terms of sharing conceptual ideas and developing their skills in applying that content?

This question is not new. However, the contemporary educational landscape makes the use of relevant and engaging teaching practices more important than ever, so much so that the Association to Advance Collegiate Schools of Business (AACSB, 2020) includes experiential learning in the accreditation standard related to student success. In a world where students have access to content through endless resources at the click of a mouse, the value of attending a lecture-focused course is being seriously questioned (Webster, 2015; Poirier, 2017). Moreover, the global, interconnected, and multi-cultural context of modern organizational life emphasizes the necessity of applied skills, particularly the misnomered "soft skills" required in working with and through others (National Association of Colleges and Employers, 2018; Organisation for Economic Co-operation and Development, 2017). What can educators do to maximize the impact of a student's educational experience so that, in addition to learning *about* the course topic, they internalize knowledge and build skills?

The Classroom as Organization (CAO) approach is an engaged teaching methodology that directly addresses this question. It is a highly experiential way of teaching, at both the undergraduate and graduate level, that enables students to become fully engaged in their learning while practicing skills. It can be used to design courses around any topic where the objective is to help students learn not only the conceptual material but also the practical skills that are associated with this knowledge.

The essence of CAO is the creation of a functioning, student-run organization. Instead of the educator taking center stage, students are placed in relevant roles of the organization, allowing them to experience organizational dynamics while learning and implementing domain-specific knowledge. As described by Cohen (1976, p. 14), the objective of CAO:

> is not to simulate an organization, but rather to create genuine organizational issues for students, to put them in the position of an organizational member who must deal with such problems as: how does work get allocated; how does one work with others who bring different expertise to tasks; how does one influence and motivate subordinates, peers and superiors; how does one cope with ambiguity in solving difficult tasks which do not have any obviously correct single answer; how can disagreements among coworkers be resolved; and how will decisions be made.

Educators drawing on the CAO approach leverage the fact that a class is an organizational system. However, the CAO approach foregrounds this and fundamentally shifts the norms of a traditional classroom. The role of student shifts from a passive recipient of teaching to that of an active organizational member. The role of educator shifts as well: from the traditional roles of presenting and testing material to that of managing and facilitating teams and individuals. In enacting their roles as employees, managers, and/or consultants, each student is empowered to affect the entire organization (class). Therefore, students present content, assess the work of their peers, and fulfill organizational functions that vary depending on the purpose of the organization.

At first glance this idea may sound similar to many experiential learning strategies, and, in truth, it is. However, CAO designs leverage experiential learning by flipping the classroom and empowering students within an authentic context. The consequence is that the classroom becomes a living laboratory where students are both participants in organizational activities and observers of their own and others' activities in the organization. CAO courses often become highly sophisticated systems that emerge, develop, and evolve over the entire term of a course. Students generate and respond to real-time organizational dynamics as they learn content-related concepts.

The purpose of this book is to serve as a comprehensive resource for educators interested in adopting CAO. The intention is to enable more people to experiment and adopt this immersive, empowering, and relational teaching methodology. This chapter provides an overview of the historical context in which CAO emerged, a summary of the learning theories that underpin the methodology, and a synthesis of the CAO literature base. Building on this foundation, Chapter 3 addresses specific considerations for using CAO, including fit with one's teaching philosophy and instructional context. Chapter 4 provides a template example of a CAO course, for those interested in adopting a CAO design for their own purposes. Finally, Chapter 5 consists of an annotated bibliography of seminal articles in the CAO literature.

2. THE EMERGENCE OF CAO

The term "Classroom as Organization" emerged within the field of organizational behavior (OB) during the creative milieu of its nascent stage. The field of OB emerged sometime in the 1960s (Dickinson, 2000) and so was not part of the earliest business schools' curricula (Milner, 2002). Business education, both in the USA and Europe, initially emphasized economics, accounting, and finance (Kast, 1965; Cheit, 1985), with a technical applied orientation in the USA and a theoretical orientation in Europe. It was not until the 1950s that behavioral science developed, led by the work of B.F. Skinner (Dickinson, 2000). Around this same time, business education in USA universities came under significant criticism (Goodrick, 2002) from independently commissioned reports from the Ford and Carnegie Foundations (i.e., Gordon and Howell, 1959; Pierson,1959, respectively). The results were consistent if not flattering: business education in the USA was perceived as low quality, narrowly vocational, and overly descriptive rather than research based. Both reports recommended increased input from the social sciences, including the disciplines of psychology, sociology, and cultural anthropology.

Attempts to integrate behavioral sciences into business education often fell flat (Cohen, 2019). The social science theory presented was perceived as complex, disconnected from organizational reality, and difficult to implement (Bradford and LeDuc, 1975; Cotton, 1975; Cohen, 1976; Clare, 1976). Early OB educators, many trained in the traditional social sciences such as psychology (Blood, 1994; Goodman and Whetten, 1998), reported that it was hard to get colleagues and students to value the contributions they could make to management education. According to Cohen (2019), "OB courses were terribly boring, and not highly regarded."

Given the many challenges regarding *what* and *how* to teach OB, a group of academics from 14 institutions gathered at the University of California, Berkeley in 1974 to share best practices in teaching organizational behavior. The gathering included a number of proponents of the T-Group (Training Group) – sensitivity training popularized through the US National Training Laboratories during the 1960s. In fact, "an astonishing number of T-group leaders were pioneers in the field of organizational behavior" (Highhouse, 2002, p. 278). This highly experiential approach to personal and group development was pioneered by Kurt Lewin and his colleagues. As described by McKeachie (1990, p. 193):

> During the 1960s, sensitivity training (T-groups, encounter groups) became the fad for high-level business executives as well as for government workers, teachers, and students. Originating in the group dynamics theories and practice of Kurt Lewin and his followers, sensitivity training groups met the 1960s generation's desire for self-analysis, confrontation of stereotypes, and overthrowing norms restricting the expression of personal needs and feelings. Many universities developed courses involving sensitivity training, and many faculty members incorporated elements of sensitivity training in conventional courses.

Key characteristics of T-groups include: (1) a situational dilemma created by a lack of structure; (2) a focus on the here-and-now; and (3) feedback loops that enable the group to learn from and about itself. Early attempts to apply the T-group process in the management classroom had varied success (Nath, 1975; Bradford and Porras, 1975); however it is possible to see the influence of the Lewinian movement in the emergence of CAO. A CAO classroom creates the situational dilemma, foregrounding and leveraging the organizational dynamics of the classroom to create a "here-and-now" common experience.

It is not surprising then, that CAO shares the T-group assumption that people can learn from the process of co-creating relational structures. But CAO departs from the loose structure of the T-group by including specific organizational structures: hierarchy, formal teams, and peer assessment serve as important feedback loops in a cycle of learning activities. It also differs in the willingness to influence the boundary conditions for the group process; the intention is for students to generate and experience organizational structures that align with specific content.

In order to better understand the CAO approach, it is helpful to foreground the teaching philosophy that underpins it: educational constructivism.

3. THE TEACHING PHILOSOPHY OF EDUCATIONAL CONSTRUCTIVISM

CAO emerged at a time when educators across many sectors of higher education were exploring the distinction between deep versus surface learning (Marton and Säljö, 1976; Dinsmore and Alexander, 2012) and the related teaching philosophy of educational constructivism (see Schneier, 1975; Magoon, 1977; Mishler, 1979). A "deep approach to learning is associated with student intention to understand and to distill meaning from the content to be learned ... The surface approach is characterized by a student's intention to cope with course requirements" (Baeten et al., 2008, p. 359). Educators play a significant role in creating the context for deep learning (Smith and Colby, 2007). A constructivist teaching philosophy is based on the assumption that students learn at their deepest level when they have opportunities to construct knowledge through their own experience and in their own terms.

The term "constructivism" holds different meanings depending on the field of application. The beginnings of educational constructivism are attributed to the work of John Dewey (i.e., pragmatism), Jean Piaget (individual and cognitive constructivism), and Lev Vygotsky (social constructivism). Dewey suggested that "active participation and self-direction by students are imperative and learner's experience and worldview are critical to problem-solving education" (Ültanır, 2012, p. 201). While theorists debate the details, there are some core ideas that underpin constructivist learning theories (Taber, 2006), including that:

• Learning is an active process undertaken by the learner constructing knowledge, not passively receiving it from an outside source.
• Although learners construct knowledge individually, it is dependent on their interaction with others and the world around them.
• Learners are not empty vessels. They bring established ideas and theories to the learning situation. Some ideas are unique to the individual learner and others, having been shaped by culture, are more broadly shared.

Constructivism directly challenges the mental model of a learner as a blank canvas on which teachers paint a body of knowledge by dictating information from the front of the classroom. Rather, in order for learning to occur, the constructivist philosophy of education posits that teachers must engage a learner's established knowledge base in order to meet the learner where they are at. This has significant implications for the role and identity of educators. The emphasis shifts away from how to deliver content and toward how best to engage learners in constructing their knowledge: this is the essence of student-centered learning (Estes, 2004). Constructivist philosophy underpins the practice of experienced-based learning (Boud et al., 2014; Dewey, 1938; Kolb, 1984; Weil and McGill, 1989), with many teaching methodologies emerging in recent years (e.g., active learning, problem-based learning, and the flipped classroom).

The CAO teaching method advocates that educators, explicitly or implicitly, incorporate constructivist assumptions into their teaching philosophy. Connecting CAO explicitly with the constructivist movement draws on a significant body of literature to support this approach to teaching. Since the introduction of constructivist education over a century ago, there is now significant evidence that meaningful learning requires active engagement and application of new information (Hake, 1998; Bransford et al., 2000; Knight and Wood, 2005; Albert and Beatty, 2014). The art and science of educating adults, andragogy (Knowles, 1980), advanced the ideas of constructivism and student-centered design by proposing that adults learn experientially, and are most engaged when solving applied problems. Three constructivist, experienced-based practices are particularly relevant to understanding CAO: authentic learning, the flipped classroom, and learning by teaching.

Authentic Learning

Authentic learning is a constructivist approach to teaching that aims to "align university teaching and learning more substantially with the way learning is achieved in real-life settings, and to base instructional methods on more authentic approaches, such as situated learning" (Herrington and Herrington, 2005, p. 3). The intention is to create learning experiences that lessen the gap between theory and practice, between knowing and doing. Drawing on the situated learning literature, Herrington and Oliver (2000) identified nine characteristics for designing authentic learning experiences that also characterize the CAO approach:

1. Authentic Context – Ensure that the physical space and context provide a "complex learning environment" (Herrington and Herrington, 2005, p. 4) that is consistent with environments where knowledge will be utilized in practice.
2. Authentic Activities – Students are challenged with "ill-defined activities that have real-world relevance, and which present complex tasks to be completed over a sustained period of time, rather than a series of shorter disconnected examples" (Herrington and Herrington, 2005, p. 5).
3. Access to Expert Performances – Exemplars of professional practice are available to enable students to learn from and model. This might involve real-world work products (i.e., memos, performance appraisal forms, etc.), interviews with experts, and/or videos of those experts' performances.
4. Multiple Roles and Perspectives – Encourage exploration of topics from different points of view.
5. Collaborative Construction of Knowledge – Group tasks are designed to require collaboration and group-level grading structures.
6. Reflection – There are formal opportunities for both individual and group-level reflection on the assigned tasks.
7. Articulation – Opportunities for students to publicly present their ideas, arguments, and thinking are included. The "very process of articulating enables formation, awareness, development and refinement of thought" (Herrington and Herrington, 2005, p. 7).

8. Coaching and Scaffolding – The teacher shifts from a didactic role to one that focuses on asking questions, and making observations, that invite students to think about their thoughts and actions: shifting from cognition to meta-cognition. In addition, other students can be a powerful resource for collaborative learning.

9. Integrated assessment of learning – Assessment is integrated with the learning activities.

By utilizing the structure of a functioning organization, CAO classrooms create an authentic context for learning about working with and through others. In particular, CAO designs replicate organizational dynamics through empowerment and interdependency.

The level of empowerment and interdependence within a particular CAO design will vary, as explored below (i.e., common elements of CAO). However, the results are predictable in two specific ways. First, empowered students become more self-reliant, more productive, and capable of increasing the amount and level of difficulty of work they can accomplish (Houghton and Neck, 2002). Additionally, students gain first-hand experience of the challenges, opportunities, and strategies for becoming more effective within complex interdependent systems. However, leveraging empowerment within an interdependent system requires time. More specifically, for students to be successful in executing authentic activities they need face-to-face time with other members of the organization. In order to focus class time on authentic activities, many CAO designs embrace the practice of flipping the classroom.

Flipped Classroom

Flipping the classroom (FTC), also referred to as the inverted classroom, is a constructivist practice that "moves the lecture outside the classroom and uses learning activities to move practice with the concepts inside the classroom" (Strayer, 2012, p. 171). The aim is for the students' first exposure to material – and the lowest level of cognitive work (i.e., gaining knowledge through transmission of information) – to move outside the classroom, reserving class time for application, analysis, and synthesis (Brame, 2013). Often technology, in the form of online videos, is used to replace traditional in-class lectures. However, the medium through which content is delivered can vary – i.e., assigned reading, PowerPoint slides (narrated or not), etc.). Abeysekera and Dawson (2015) explain FTC broadly as "a set of pedagogical approaches that:

1. move most information-transmission teaching out of class; 2. use class time for learning activities that are active and social; and 3. require students to complete pre- and/or post-class activities to fully benefit from in class work" (p. 3).

FTC is an active-learning approach that engages the student with the material they are learning. The range of in-class activities employed is as broad as the imagination of the educator. It includes any and all experiential learning strategies: large group discussions, interactive quizzes using clicker response technologies, traditional quizzes, small group activities (e.g., cases, problems, role plays, etc., think-pair-share activities, student presentations, debates, etc.), and simulations. Van Alten et al. (2019) concluded that "students in flipped classrooms achieve significantly higher assessed learning outcomes than students in traditional classrooms" (p. 15). Two factors specifically leverage this ability of FTC: maintaining the amount of face-to-face time in the classroom, and utilizing quizzes (van Alten et al., 2019). In this way, FTC complements the CAO approach by reserving class time for the authentic activities described above.

Research on student satisfaction with FTC is varied. Drawing on self-determination theory (Ryan and Deci, 2000), Abeysekera and Dawson (2015) suggest that FTC methodologies contribute to greater intrinsic and extrinsic motivation by satisfying learners' needs for competence, autonomy, and relatedness. Despite claims that FTC contributes to greater student satisfaction (Mason et al., 2013), meta-analyses of empirical evidence suggest a more measured assertion: FTC does not negatively impact student satisfaction ratings (van Alten et al., 2019). This may be in part because students vary in their self-regulated learning (SRL) capability, and those who are unfamiliar with the increased importance, and responsibility, of preparing for class may need time to adjust to new classroom norms (Mason et al., 2013; Lo et al., 2017). However, another meta-analysis found that students increase SRL capabilities more in flipped classrooms than in traditional classrooms (Tan et al., 2017). There is of course a learning curve in implementing any new methodology, both for the educator and the students, and the nuances of FTC are no exception. As FTC becomes more established, both educators and students will gain competence with the practice. In the interim, it seems decreased satisfaction does not mean decreased learning. For example, in a quasi-experimental design, Missildine et al. (2013) found that students in the FTC group had higher examination scores but lower satisfaction with the teaching method.

Evidence suggests that FTC does foster greater peer-to-peer and student-to-educator interaction (Bergmann and Sams, 2012; Sun and Wu, 2016; Yu and Wang, 2016; Zainuddin and Attaran, 2016). One of the ways that CAO designs encourage such interaction is by including the practice of learning by teaching.

Learning by Teaching

Learning by teaching includes the cooperative learning strategies (e.g. Slavin, 1983) of peer teaching and assessment. As described by Topping (1996): "People from similar social groups who are not professional teachers [are] helping each other learn and learning themselves by teaching" (p. 322). Students learn from and with each other in both formal and informal ways (Boud et al., 2014). For example, informal peer learning takes place outside the classroom when a learner asks a fellow student for help. CAO formalizes peer learning through the intentional strategies of peer teaching and assessment. The benefits include increased skill in: working with others; critical enquiry and reflection; communication and articulation of knowledge, understanding, and skills; managing learning and how to learn; and self- and peer assessment (Boud, 2001).

Peer teaching maximizes student responsibility for learning and enhances cooperative and social skills (Goldschmid and Goldschmid, 1976). The act of preparing to teach requires students to pay more attention to the material and organize it in a meaningful way (Carberry and Ohland, 2012), and the teaching act itself can deepen understanding of the material (Fiorella and Mayer, 2013; Okita et al., 2013; Koh et al., 2018). Taking a teaching role can improve attitudes toward life-long learning (Peng et al., 2019) and teamwork skills (Zhou et al., 2019). There is evidence that peer teachers may have greater influence in shifting learners' pre-existing beliefs (Chrispeels et al., 2019). This is helpful in addressing the constructivist assumption that learners can carry established ideas that are inaccurate and/or inconsistent with scientific understanding.

Peer assessment "is an arrangement for learners to consider and specify the level, value, or quality of a product or performance of other equal status learners" (Topping, 2009, p. 20). Wide variation in the use of peer assessment (also referred to as peer grading, peer evaluation, peer review, peer feedback and peer interaction) means there are few absolutes within the literature (Topping, 1998; Ashenafi, 2017; Kollar and Fischer, 2010; Strijbos and Sluijsmans, 2010). Variables for consideration in peer-assessment designs include whether it is: formative or summative;

one-off or iterative; mutual or anonymous; verbal and/or written; individual, dyadic, or group-based; and delivered inside or outside of class time. Regardless of the design, developing peer-assessment skills through scaffolded training is a critical success factor for learning (Topping, 2009; van Zundert et al., 2010; Könings et al., 2019). One of the benefits of peer assessment is the potential for greater amounts of formative assessment (i.e., assessment *for* learning as opposed to assessment *of* learning) by expanding the source of that feedback from the teacher to members of the whole class. In addition, peer assessment results in cognitive gains for both the assessor and the assessed (Topping, 2005). In their meta-analysis of studies comparing peer and teacher marks, Falchikov and Goldfinch (2000) concluded that, on average, there was agreement between peer and teacher assessments. They also concluded that agreement was more likely when there were well-specified assessment criteria that were both student-defined and well-understood.

However, both peer assessment and peer teaching need to be carefully structured to be efficient (Fischer et al., 2013; King, 2002; Michinov et al., 2015). The quality and impact of peer teaching can be improved with structures that require meaningful interaction between the students (Roscoe, 2014): in other words, structuring the teaching assignment so that students move beyond summarizing the material and instead teach by "generating inferences and actively reflecting upon [their] own understanding of the material" (Fiorella and Mayer, 2016, p. 729). Similarly, the structure of providing a feedback template with pre-specified and mutually discussed criteria can significantly increase the quantity and quality of peer assessment (Gielen and De Wever, 2015).

In summary, CAO is a teaching approach that draws on multiple teaching practices from the constructivist paradigm: authentic learning, the flipped classroom, and learning by teaching. However, the early pioneers of the CAO methodology were experimenting with the precursors to these practices long before they were named with these labels. The next section outlines the contributions from these CAO pioneers, and then explores the variations and adaptations that have evolved.

4. THE BEGINNINGS AND EXPANSION OF CAO

There are four primary contributions in the early CAO literature: Bradford and LeDuc (1975), Cotton (1975), Cohen (1976), and Clare (1976). These seminal articles, appearing in the first two years of *The*

Teaching of Organizational Behavior journal, each called for a departure from the traditional student and teacher roles. These pioneers were experimenting with different strategies for teaching an applied subject. Each model went beyond using experiential activities, and made the classroom a living organization. Their articles describe how their CAO functioned, the elements that were successful, and the difficulties they encountered. These are not empirical articles, as the authors' primary intention was to share their designs to encourage more creative implementation of CAO. Of the four original CAO designs, three focused on small groups where students completed team-level assignments related to the content of the course (Bradford and LeDuc, 1975; Cohen, 1976; Clare, 1976). In contrast, Cotton created a functioning hierarchical organization with a defined output. The four designs, in chronological order of publication, include:

- a "two-tier" design that linked a first-year MBA OB course with a second-year MBA OB course and utilized a small group, discussion-based model (Bradford and LeDuc);
- a hierarchical design that included functional departments with an external focus for the organization – a resume distribution service for graduating students (Cotton);
- a small group design where assignments were completed in teams, peer assessment was utilized, and the team leader met with the professor regularly (Cohen);
- a course design that extended Cohen's model by incorporating differentiated roles within teams and a more elaborate peer-assessment scheme (Clare).

Although all four of these CAO models evolved around the same time, there seems to have been little if any collaboration between the authors. Much of the literature cites Cohen as the initiator of CAO, although a careful review of the literature reveals that the other models have been equally influential.

Over the next few decades, CAO methodologies proliferated by building on the ideas put forth by these first four works. Each article on CAO demonstrates how the author(s) created an organization by integrating the broad topic of the course with specific organizational concepts in order to allow students to live within and learn from certain organizational realities. In a myriad of ways, they adopted the perspective of manager and consultant to view the classroom as an opportunity to create organizational dynamics that matched their learning objectives. While there are many nuances, the following categories are helpful in understanding the CAO literature: the interdependent organization versus leadered group design (André, 2011); the external versus internal focus of CAO; various adaptations; and, finally, broad common elements.

Interdependent Organization vs. Leadered Group Design

In the four seminal articles the basic tenet of CAO was present: create an organization within the classroom. While each was unique, they can be organized in three categories (Figure 2.1), two of which have continued to evolve over time in the literature: interdependent organization CAO (Cotton, 1975) and small group-based CAO, also called leadered group design (Cohen, 1976; Clare, 1976).

In Figure 2.1 *interdependent organization* is a label to describe designs that focus on creating an organization in which each group is assigned responsibilities that affect the whole organization: groups are dependent on one another to produce their final product or service. *Leadered group* is a label to describe designs that focus on small groups; this often involves giving specific roles to group members, including manager or team leader. In the leadered group design, each group is given an assignment to do; and, although they must work together to produce the assignment, their efforts are not dependent upon, nor do they impact, other teams.

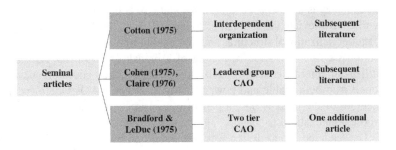

Figure 2.1   *Seminal CAO articles: interdependent organization v. leadered group design*

The first published example of the interdependent organization design was from Cotton, who created a hierarchical organizational structure for his CAO. The organization ran a resume distribution service which included the "maximum number of business functions and operate[d] in realistic ways" (Cotton, 1975, p. 25). The goal was to create a business with real output in order to engage students in all levels and functions of the business. Cotton's intention was to enable students to experience organizational behavior within the reality of life in a hierarchical organization. Students were placed in teams with built-in interdependence with the whole organization. For example, the sales/marketing team was responsible for the sale of the product but had to work interdependently with all other teams to ensure successful delivery of that product. Cotton, utilizing the interdependent organization model, went to great lengths to mimic the realities of a functioning hierarchy. For example, only managers were allowed to speak with the CEO (the educator). He found that his design so closely reflected the realities of a strict hierarchy that he also recreated the realities of a disenfranchised working class at the bottom of the pyramid.

In the end, Cotton declares this design a "disaster" because it was too realistic: students in management positions had a great experience, while students occupying lower-level positions were frustrated, disempowered, and disillusioned. His article provides evidence that CAOs can indeed mimic organizational realities, giving students insight into how organizations work and the opportunity to develop the requisite skills. However, Cotton's conclusion regarding the limitation of creating a hierarchical bureaucracy is a valid concern. Subsequent CAOs based on his example worked to alleviate the difficulties found in a strict hierarchy by creating flatter organizational structures and/or meaningful roles for each student. Cotton's CAO marks the beginning of a branch of CAO models that utilize an interdependent organization design. Other educators have found it to be a viable and powerful way to design CAOs where each member of the class is both a part of a department and linked into the whole organization.

The leadered group design was first published by Cohen (1976) and quickly adapted by Clare (1976). In these examples of the leadered group design, the emphasis was on role differentiation within the team. There was no built-in interaction or dependencies between teams. In this design, all output comes at the group level, not the organizational level, and each group acts independently of other groups. Specific roles were assigned to individual group members, including a group manager, to ensure that each student took responsibility for some aspect of the assignments and that all group-level tasks were completed. The educator fulfilled the role of the organization's senior manager by meeting with team managers regularly to provide feedback and assess the quality of the group output. Students were held accountable to their group via peer assessment, feedback from their team manager, and assessment of individual work by the senior manager.

While Bradford and LeDuc's two-tier CAO is part of the seminal literature and was published around the same time as the other articles, only one subsequent CAO article builds upon it directly. Bradford and LeDuc created a design to accommodate 300 MBA students in an introductory-level course while leveraging the advanced Master of Business Studies (MBS) students as discussion leaders in the introductory MBA course. Lectures delivered by the professor were used for part of the introductory course. In addition, the discussion groups facilitated deeper and more individualized learning for MBA students, as well as a chance for MBA students to lead in an organizational context. The only other article in the literature that builds on this model modifies the design to an undergraduate course (Graf and Couch, 1984).

The labels of interdependent organization versus leadered group design help name an important and enduring distinction within the CAO literature. However, the evolution of CAO designs is not captured with this single categorization.

External vs. Internal Focus

Another important distinction between CAO designs is the direction of focus for the organization's purpose: external or internal. Externally focused CAO designs deliver a product or service outside of the organization. This might include running a community event or designing and implementing a business for external stakeholders. Within externally focused CAOs, students are typically organized into functional groups in order to successfully deliver a product or service to customers. Internally focused CAO designs deliver the service of leveraging individual and collective learning from the dynamics that occur within the organization as members take responsibility for teaching the subject of the course. Within internally focused CAOs, activities focus on both deep learning of content and the execution of organizational tasks that occur at the team and/or whole organization level. For both external and internal CAO designs, reflection and learning about group and organizational dynamics emerges from action: either product/service delivery, peer teaching and assessment, or some combination of both.

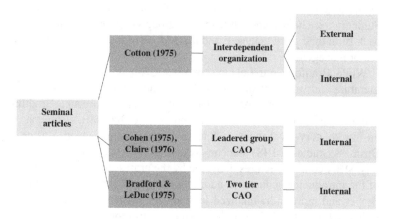

Figure 2.2   *Seminal CAO articles: internal v. external designs*

Figure 2.2 provides a simplified picture of how the CAO literature has evolved in relation to the two key distinctions discussed thus far: (1) interdependent organization versus leadered group, and (2) internal versus external focus. All of the leadered group designs in the CAO literature, dating back to the seminal articles by Cohen (1976) and Clare (1976), are internally focused. The key stakeholders are the members of the organization (i.e., class) and the focus is on the learning of course material. In contrast, the interdependent organization designs in the CAO literature, instigated by Cotton (1975), include both internal and external foci (Figure 2.3).

In the externally focused interdependent organization designs of CAO there are two main models: create a business (Randolph and Miles, 1979; Miller, 1991; Goltz, 1992) and event planning (Sheehan et al., 2009; McDonald et al., 2011). In the *create a business* external design, Randolph and Miles present a series of simulations in which students, placed in functional groups of an organization, are asked to solve problems presented to them. The students act as an organization while solving business problems and are subsequently scored by the professor on their solutions. Oddou (1987) builds on this model, integrating a semester-long simulation of a hierarchical business that requires students to fabricate and sell fake circuit boards. The process is simplified since the students

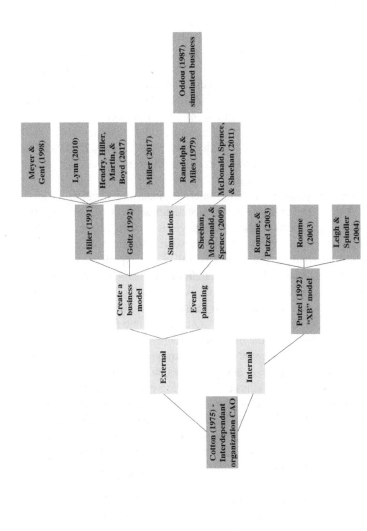

Figure 2.3   Evolution of CAO literature from Cotton (1975)

do not actually create and run a real business, but work through a simulated business model over the semester. Goltz (1992) creates a hierarchical organization with the goal of creating a college survival guide tailored to their university.

The most prolific of these external create a business designs originates with Miller's (1991, 2017) Management 101 Project out of Bucknell University. Miller's model of CAO is an external interdependent organization design where student groups plan, organize, and run a for-profit business during the course of a semester. The class meets three times a week for regular lecture-style teaching, and twice a week in a lab where groups plan, organize, and run the business. The topics of this course are carefully orchestrated so students learn what they need to know at each stage of the business. This design has been running continuously for 30 years at Bucknell University (Hendry et al., 2017; Miller, 2017) and has been the inspiration for creative iterations at other universities (Meyer and Gent, 1998; Lynn, 2010).

Another long-running external interdependent organization design is an event-management CAO in which students are in charge of managing and marketing a sports festival (Sheehan et al., 2009). This model, which has been running consecutively for 17 years, integrates theory and soft skills through traditional teaching as well as the experience of planning and managing the actual event. In addition to enabling students to practice management and organizational skills, this model facilitates interesting opportunities for students to partner with university-wide events.

While the external designs of CAO take multiple forms, there is only one published model of the internal interdependent organization design: Putzel's (1992) eXperiential Based Learning (XB). Putzel's internal interdependent organization design focuses on the interpersonal dynamics of accomplishing work through others in a complex organization. The purpose of the organization is to create individual- and organization-level learning: students are tasked to teach specific content, provide feedback, assess learning, oversee the overall functioning of the class, and recommend final grades. Students work in teams that have interdependent functions. In addition, each student has a unique role with specific responsibilities, often with organization-wide influence. Putzel's model has been utilized in a handful of universities and has spawned a number of research articles (Romme and Putzel, 2003; Putzel, 1992; Bright et al., 2012; Leigh and Spindler, 2004).

Cotton's original design includes five levels of hierarchy and Putzel employs three levels. The authors of this book have created their own design of CAO, building on Putzel's model while simplifying it significantly for the first-time user. This design, outlined in Chapter 4, simplifies the hierarchy in favor of emphasizing the self-organizing and positive organizational dynamics that are possible. The aim is to give students the opportunity to be a part of a highly functional system in the hope that they will know when they experience it again in the workplace, and even work toward recreating it.

Romme (2003) adapts Putzel's internal interdependent organization CAO for the purpose of chairing multiple masters projects concurrently. This CAO, referred to as a thesis ring, has the goal of providing a supervisory relationship to students who are completing a master degree thesis. Whereas students usually meet one-on-one with their chair during this process, Romme invites five to seven students with thesis topics that are in the same discipline to be a part of a thesis ring. In addition to significant responsibilities related to peer editing, students share the rotating roles of meeting chair and/or scribe. The thesis ring meets every three weeks, when students, as well as the educator, provide feedback on each other's writing. The members of the thesis ring are empowered to make the final decision regarding whether a thesis has been successfully defended. The learning emphasis is on the skills of critical thinking, writing, and discipline-related concepts. CAO thesis rings are ongoing presently in six European universities (Romme and Putzel, 2003) and are fostering ongoing research (van Seggelen-Damen and Romme, 2014).

In summary, these works demonstrate how the CAO literature contains internally and externally focused designs, both of which have merit depending on the purpose for which they are used. The external format (Cotton, 1975; Miller, 1991) facilitates a realistic experience of serving external stakeholders and the necessary interdependence of functional departments (i.e., marketing, sales, product design, etc.). On the other hand, the internal model enables an increased attention to and exploration of the interpersonal realities of an organizational environment (Putzel, 1992). Of the interdependent organization design, the Management 101 Project's external and XB's internal CAOs have been the most influential. For instance, each has inspired subsequent related articles and have been adopted at other universities. However, there are interesting differences between the Management 101 Project and XB that illustrate some of the many nuances contained in the CAO literature: the Management

101 Project presents the content through traditional lecture-style class sessions – students apply concepts during lab time; XB uses the organizational design to make students responsible for presenting course content. Both designs reflect their respective course content and objectives. The Management 101 Project emphasizes the various business functions as well as management skills within these functions. The XB course focuses on the organizational realities of getting things done through others. Despite both Miller and Putzel using the interdependent organization CAO design, each adapted it to their unique context. This is common in the CAO literature, and therefore makes it challenging to distill simple categorizations.

Variations and Adaptations

Beyond the distinctions discussed above, there are many variations and adaptations within the CAO literature. It is difficult to summarize these in a simple table because of the nuances within and overlap between individual contributions. However, four themes emerge as one way to understand this literature: students designing elements of the course; instructors creating content variations; simulations that involve splitting the class; and in-depth attention to particular developmental aspects. The majority of these adaptations come from the small group or leadered group designs of CAO (Cohen, 1976; Clare, 1976), as can be seen in Figure 2.4.

The first theme in the CAO literature relates to articles that emphasize the processes of empowering and guiding students in making many of the decisions about course policy and structure: What textbook will be used? How many tests will there be and when will they be scheduled? What assignments will students undertake and how will they be graded? The focus is on partnering with students to design the learning experience and creating a course with full engagement. The organizational learning comes through designing the class and then implementing the design together. These processes are found in both undergraduate (Weil, 1988) and MBA courses (Brown and Murti, 2003).

The second theme in the CAO literature concerns how to utilize the method to teach different content areas, including policy (Balke, 1981), oral and written communication skills (Finan, 1992), and high-commitment management (Lawrence, 1992). Balke provides an entire course design for a policy course which could be adapted to different topics. He utilizes functional departments as well as individ-

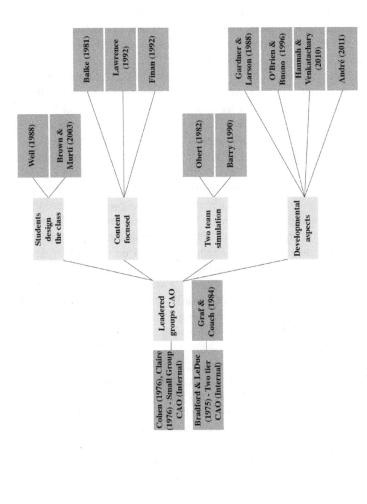

Figure 2.4   CAO literature: leadered groups

ual roles within groups. Balke runs class time as a meeting within an organization, often having students present content, lead discussions, or take part in debates. Finan redesigned a traditionally taught communications course into a CAO course, focusing on developmental learning in a number of practical business-related skills. Lawrence demonstrates how to build CAO around a particular theory (in this case high-commitment management theory). She systematically describes the tenets of high-commitment management and how she implements those principles in this graduate-level human resources (HR) course. These articles illustrate that it is possible to adapt CAO to accommodate various course topics and offer practical insight into how this is accomplished.

The third theme in the CAO literature relates to designs that split the class into two groups in order to extract learning opportunities from a combination of observation, experience, and reflection. In Obert's (1982) design, the two groups compete on assigned tasks during a series of simulations. The resulting competition, tension, and conflict are leveraged to teach about change, influence, and power. Barry (1990) also splits the class in half. While one group completes a complex task the other group observes them: the observing group acts as a consulting organization and prepares a report based on their analysis. The teams switch these responsibilities back and forth throughout the semester.

The fourth theme concerns articles that focus on a particular developmental aspect. André (2011) emphasizes the importance of rotating leadership responsibilities to ensure all students get to practice leading and assessing their peers' skills, while O'Brien and Buono (1996) highlight the importance of supporting group development and share a framework for intentionally experiencing and learning from management roles. Gardner and Larson (1988) specifically address a number of problems encountered in CAO, such as "the selection of team members, non-performing team members, peer grading, and student attitudes and abilities in handling group work" (p. 13). The authors share procedures, policies, and practices to address these issues. These course designs illustrate how developmental aspects can be emphasized through the CAO methodology.

The themes identified above summarize some of the similarities found within the CAO literature and demonstrate the many ways that CAO has been implemented and developed. Drawing on the distinctions discussed thus far (i.e., interdependent organization versus leadered group, internal versus external focus, and the four themes), Figures 2.5a and 2.5b provide a picture of key articles in the CAO literature. However, each article contains interesting nuances and complexities that are not captured with this simplification. Given the impossibility of a simple summary, what are the common elements to a successful CAO?

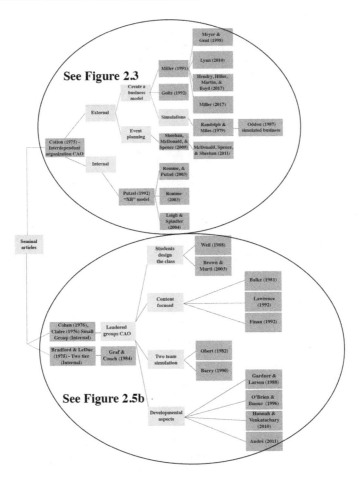

Figure 2.5a   CAO literature: the full picture

5.   COMMON ELEMENTS IN CAO

Recognizing the diversity of both published and unpublished CAO designs, Romme and Putzel (2003) suggested five principles as boundary

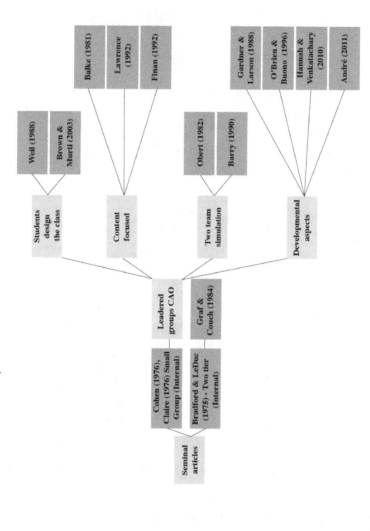

Figure 2.5b   CAO literature: the full picture

conditions for a CAO design. In this section, their "design-in-the-large" (p. 513) principles are updated and adapted in order to discuss the CAO literature: (1) leverage interdependence; (2) utilize peer assessment; (3) give students both learning and management roles; (4) delegate as a senior manager; and (5) balance structure and ambiguity to support learning. Although presented as five distinct elements that define CAO, as with most teaching practices, these are interrelated: they happen all together in real time. Furthermore, each educator emphasizes or deemphasizes certain points depending on their course objectives and preferred teaching style.

Element #1: Leverage Interdependence

Interdependence involves an "organizational relationship where individuals are assigned ... roles where they are required to share the inputs, throughputs and outputs of their work" (Yakubovich and Burg, 2019, p. 1014). Interdependence is ubiquitous in organizational life requiring coordination between individuals, between individuals and teams, between teams, and so on (Worren, 2018). Interdependence is a distinguishing factor between team-based learning and the CAO approach. Team-based learning assigns the same task to different teams: task differentiation between the teams is low; task differentiation within each team varies depending on their process and the instructions received from the educator. There is little need to collaborate with people outside one's assigned team in order to meet the learning objective of working collaboratively to generate team project work. There is a fundamental shift when each team description includes a unique element of inter-team task interdependence: a specific but unique task is assigned to that team, which requires the team to work with organizational members beyond the team in order to successfully accomplish their responsibilities.

Romme and Putzel (2003; also Romme, 2003) emphasize the importance of building interdependence into the organization to recreate some of the complicated dynamics that occur naturally in organizations. They advocate for class-wide interdependence, meaning that each team has responsibilities that impact the whole organization. Forming interdependent relationships between students and teams is a powerful tool to create an authentic organization that is central in CAO designs.

Early CAO designs created a level of interdependence within teams, but did not create organization-wide interdependence between those teams. For example, Cohen (1976) used a leadered group design with managers and gave each group tasks that they completed concurrently. Similarly, Clare (1976) used the leadered group design, adding specific roles for each person within the team to increase interdependence and personal responsibility. Both of these designs demonstrate that while the leadered group model does not support class-wide interdependence, group-level interdependence can be built in by creating roles for individuals in the group. These early CAO models were criticized because the leadered group design fails to introduce the organization-wide interdependence that is necessary for students to experience authentic organizational interactions (Pendse, 1984; Barry, 1990).

Pendse proposed that, to become an authentic organization, groups need to have distinct roles that affect the whole organization in such a way that they cannot be successful unless the entire organization coordinates efforts. Barry identified interdependence between groups to be one of the necessary features for CAOs to be relevant and applicable to learning business skills. He proposed that interdependence creates the need to work together across teams to produce products and services. Barry's Twincorp design is created from a conglomeration of small group design (Cohen, 1976), consultancy approach (Tubbs, 1985), and the split halves organizational development approach (Obert, 1982; Steenberg and Gillette, 1984) in an attempt to replicate the realities of an authentic organization. For the classroom to act as an authentic organization, interdependence must be created from the beginning and reinforced throughout the course. Whole class interdependence will create the most robust and interesting authentic organizational interactions (Putzel, 1992; Romme and Putzel, 2003).

In an effort to create greater authenticity, some CAO designs are based on highly interdependent hierarchical organizations that provide the requisite complexity (Cotton, 1975; Putzel, 1992). While Cotton created a five-level hierarchical organization to produce a resume service for seniors, Putzel created an internal design with three levels of hierarchy to teach OB. However, these designs also replicate some of the difficulties and weaknesses of the hierarchical organization. Many other organizational forms exist that can be utilized to create CAOs with the interdependence of an authentic organization, and will be further discussed in subsequent chapters.

The importance of students learning to function and thrive in interdependent teams is evident in the business community. A CAO classroom with interdependent teams offers realistic practice that will transfer to the business context (Barry, 1990; Sheehan et al., 2009). While traditional methodologies teach students to be passive consumers of information, the interdependent, authentic organization design requires that they fully engage, influence one another, and work together to succeed in the classroom (Oddou,1987). However, it is important to understand that replicating managerial reality with intentional interdependence is also related to the disorientation and frustration that students can have in CAO (Mezoff et al., 1979). The experience of increased intensity (Sleeth and Brown, 1984), turbulence (Leigh and Spindler, 2004), fear, and frustration (Oddou, 1987; Mezoff in Mezoff et al., 1979) is well documented. In short, while interdependence is central to creating a CAO design and replicating organizational realities, it is not easy for students or educators. The creation of interdependence, along with deciding how to deal with the resulting tensions, must be recognized and planned for early in the design process (e.g. Mezoff et al., 1979).

Whether the organization is a leadered group design (e.g. Cohen, 1975) or an interdependent organization design (e.g. Cotton, 1976; Miller, 1991; Putzel, 1992), or whether it has an internal or external focus, the purpose is to foreground and utilize the dynamics of an authentic, functioning organization in the classroom, which necessitates creating interdependence throughout the organization.

Element #2: Utilize Peer Assessment

Students are the primary resource in any CAO design and planning how to utilize them will significantly boost the efficacy of the learning environment. Romme and Putzel (2003) encourage us to "acknowledge and involve students as potential supervisors, team leaders, co-teachers, co assessors, and so forth" (p. 525). This represents an effective use of human resources as well as utilizing empowerment principles, all great ways to model positive organizational dynamics in CAO (Romme and Putzel, 2003). Peer assessment has been part of CAO models from the beginning (Bradford and LeDuc, 1975; Cotton, 1975; Cohen, 1976; Clare, 1976), and continues to be a core element of CAO designs. Peer assessment is valuable for student learning since it provides multiple perspectives on student work, offering more feedback than an educator alone could provide. Furthermore, learning to assess others' work and provide meaningful feedback is a valuable skill to develop for the workforce. CAO proponents point out that despite the reticence of students to assess one another, valuable managerial skills are developed through this aspect of the course (Mezoff et al., 1979). Both informal peer assessment (i.e., formative feedback) and formal peer assessment that is part of the summative grading system will be further explored in this section.

Feedback is a form of informal peer assessment that is critical for effective CAOs. Bright and Turesky (2010) argue that feedback is one of the foundational tools that "helps students generate a powerful, flourishing, and dynamic classroom experience" (p. 2). They suggest that the benefits of feedback to the CAO classroom include that it: (1) enables students to make sense of their shared experiences; (2) fosters bonding and self-organizing which increases their ownership of the experience as well as increasing accountability; and (3) increases the amount and quality of feedback given to each student from what the educator alone could provide. For it to be effective both positive and constructive feedback is needed. Bright and Turesky intentionally teach students the feedback process and provide examples of feedback templates that they use in their CAO to guide the process. Hendry et al. (2017) also intentionally teach students how to give feedback by focusing on non-defensive communication strategies to encourage open-minded thinking. They intentionally model these skills in the classroom while giving feedback to students or teams.

CAO utilizes peer-to-peer feedback more extensively than other constructivist methods (Bright et al., 2016). The skill of giving and receiving feedback is valuable in the workplace and features prominently in CAO designs (e.g., Bradford, 1975; Gardner and Larson, 1988; Bright and Turesky, 2010; Hannah and Venkatachary, 2010; André, 2011; Bright et al., 2012, 2016; Hendry et al., 2017). Specific strategies include incorporating feedback into written assignments, presentations, managerial or team-based skills, or other course deliverables. Feedback can also be given at different levels: individuals within teams can provide feedback to one another; teams can give feedback to other teams; or the whole class can give feedback on presentations or teamwork (e.g. Putzel, 1992; Bright et al., 2016; Gardner and Larson, 1988). Furthermore, receiving personal feedback from multiple sources gives each student insight and data for reflection that can prove valuable in their personal and professional growth, enhancing the depth of learning.

While formative assessment is an important part of CAO design, summative peer assessment is also used consistently. The early authors of CAO utilized summative peer assessment as a part of the grading system in their leadered group designs (Bradford and LeDuc, 1975; Cohen, 1976; Clare, 1976). Cohen had a fairly simple peer-assessment system where the team manager assigned grades to team members for one major assignment. Clare created a more elaborate system with different weights of peer grading for managers and non-managers. Putzel (1992) created a complex evaluation system in which students collected and organized hundreds of assessment data points for each student which were used to recommend end-of-semester grades. While some authors dedicate a small percentage of the grade to peer assessment (e.g., Balke, 1981), with the majority of the final grade determined by educator-assessed work, Putzel's model is 100 percent peer assessed.

While CAO practitioners advocate for peer grading as an effective form of learning, and as a source of student engagement and motivation, they also recognize that it causes a certain amount of student anxiety. Mezoff et al. (1979) found that formal peer assessment stifled enthusiasm for their course. Cohen (in Mezoff et al., 1979) argues that peer assessment is an important business skill that students must master to become effective: the peer-assessment process builds trust and cohesion in teams, creating higher levels of team accomplishment. Educators need to address student reticence toward peer grading from the beginning as benefits are worth the effort involved in helping students overcome their fears.

Element #3: Give Students both Learning and Management Roles

For CAO to become a flourishing organization that offers the opportunity for deep learning experiences, students must have learning and man-agement roles, both of which are directly related to Kolb's Experiential Learning Theory. Learning, according to Kolb (1984), is "the process whereby knowledge is created through the transformation of experience. Knowledge results from the combination of grasping and transforming experience" (p. 41). The management role gives students the impetus to be actors, attempting to influence others in order to succeed in their assigned role. The learning role encourages students to reflect on the complex set of interactions and outcomes happening in the classroom. Reflecting serves the purpose of allowing them to construct their understanding of the course content as well as offering the opportunity to adjust their behavior and develop skills. In this way, the active role of manager and the reflective role of learner are constantly in play for each member of the class. Translated into Kolb's definition of learning, the manager role creates experiences, while the reflective learning role assists students in grasping and transforming that experience into usable, actionable knowledge.

Educators must carefully design student roles to have both an active influencing component (i.e., manager role) and a reflective learning component in order to leverage organizational interactions for deep learning. When students attempt to enact their roles, they discover the authority of the role alone does not always produce the desired influence; through a combination of reflection and coaching, they can explore various influence tactics to get work done (Romme and Putzel, 2003). A CAO that integrates the manager and learner roles not only sets a foundation for experiential learning to flourish, but also sets the stage for the interdependent relationships that create an authentic learning context. Student roles that combine both learning and managerial responsibilities result in powerful learning experiences that integrate theory and practice.

Management roles are not confined to being group leaders. Although some designs designate group leaders, ideally every student in the class has a role that specifies something that they manage. The form of the management role differs according to the CAO design. In leadered group designs the students' management roles are within their teams (e.g. Cohen, 1976; Clare, 1976). In the interdependent organization design there are also management roles that extend to the whole organization. This expands the management experience from influencing only the group to influencing a complex organization. In the externally focused interdependent organization design, where students are running a business or providing a service, the management roles fall into functional groups; each functional group has specific responsibilities and must work with the whole organization to produce the product or service.

The leadered group and externally focused CAO designs rely on the lecture format for teaching course concepts (e.g. Cohen, 1976; Clare, 1976; Miller, 1991; Lawrence, 1992) while emphasizing the management role for students in small teams or functional groups. Students take in the material from the educator and are able to then apply that knowledge in their teamwork or external project. Although this is the norm in CAO designs, the opportunity to engage students more deeply in their learning role is often overlooked. Putzel (1992) assigns each team the managerial responsibility of teaching the material, and specifies that they must utilize an experiential format; they cannot lecture. This creates a management role for students by tasking them with peer teaching. It also has the potential to increase student engagement in the course. Although students are not initially as adept at teaching content as educators, this unleashes student creativity and motivation, and by mid-semester students can lead impressive learning activities.

There are many ways to ensure that the management roles in CAO are taken seriously and that students gain the most benefit possible from these roles. Finan (1992) uses a matching process to create pairs of fourth-year and first-year students where the former act as managers. These pairs collaborate to learn assigned content and also contribute as part of other teams (e.g., briefings, business presentations, providing feedback). Josefowitz (1978) addresses the reticence undergraduates have to lead one another in groups while also emphasizing the important learning that can happen through the selection of people for manage- ment roles. She notes that assigned group leaders often abdicate their leadership in favor of being liked and supporting social conventions. She develops a modified form of what she calls "assessment centers"; managers are elected and subsequently build their own teams from class members through an interactive interview and hiring process. Josefowitz finds that students are more engaged and take their roles more seriously with this methodology.

Regardless of the content focus, business students require the skills to work with and through people. As discussed above, Andre (2011) rotates student leadership so that each student has the opportunity to lead as well as to receive feedback. The result is that more students get "the opportunity to lead, responsibility to lead well, accountability for leader- ship effectiveness and feedback on leadership technique" (p. 601). Goltz (1992), similarly to Andre, implements a rotating management scheme in her course and finds that, although it does disrupt group functioning to some extent, the benefit of students experiencing various leadership styles throughout the semester outweighs the inconvenience.

There are different ways to implement management roles in teams and across the whole organization, as well as specific tactics to organize and emphasize the management role. One important discovery from the literature is that most CAOs do not fully leverage peer teaching for management purposes. Putzel's (1992) example of making students responsible for teaching content in an experiential manner enhances both the student's management role and the depth of content learning. Bright et al. (2016) research the impact of students creating and presenting course content on their learning outcomes, and conclude that creating content positively affects student content knowledge and engagement.

Element #4: Delegate Power and Responsibility

Another point of discussion throughout the CAO literature is the shift in the role of educator from teacher to manager. Traditionally, the educator orchestrates the classroom activities. In contrast, CAO puts students in charge of much of the learning process by taking a more student-centered approach (Conklin, 2013; Bright and Turesky, 2010). The first three design principles illustrate specific ways in which the power dynamic shifts. In design principle one, leverage interdependence, power is shifted to the students through role descriptions that include many of the responsibilities that are usually held by the educator. Power is also shifted away from the educator through the second design principle, utilizing peer-to-peer feedback: the responsibility of assessment is shifted, at least in part, from the educator to the students. Giving students management roles, design principle three, redirects the power dynamics by assigning students managerial and decision-making responsibilities. Every element of the CAO design shifts normal classroom power dynamics between educators and students.

One way to describe this shift in power is empowerment: a motivational process involving the sharing of power with subordinates through a leader's actions and/or organizational structures (Conger and Kanungo, 1988). Empowerment results in a greater ability to work autonomously (Amundsen and Martinsen, 2014), enhanced engagement with and meaning of work (Spreitzer, 1995), and increased self-efficacy (Thomas and Velthouse, 1990). Empowerment is widely adopted in organizations (Lee and Edmondson, 2017; van Baarle et al., 2019), which supports the authenticity of designing classroom experiences that enable students to practice being empowered agents.

This shift in power in CAO is an effective force for learning, and it can also be an uncomfortable experience for all involved. While students are less adept at performing their assigned roles than educators, the process of learning that happens while attempting to fulfill their role is effective. However, students are uncomfortable as they are asked to take on responsibilities that stretch them and that make them feel incompetent. Similarly, for the educator, becoming a manager and coach to students can be both destabilizing and create a sense of vulnerability. Instead of a clear and organized class session, the educator needs to be prepared to encounter multiple unknown situations and use coaching and management tactics to leverage and transform the experience into meaningful learning. Mezoff et al. (1979) lauded CAO as one of his most significant learning experiences personally and professionally, while at the same time expressing his hesitation to move away from being the content expert because of his fear that the students would see the course as "soft" and not take it seriously. Acknowledging the fear and anxiety that can be aroused, Conklin (2013, p. 254) asks:

> how might we muster the courage to stand close to the edge, an edge where even we may tremble at the prospect of not knowing what will be learned or how a class session or term will turn out? Giving over the control and unleashing the potential of the unknown may likely be met with similar levels of courage in our students.

However, the literature reveals that many CAOs still rely on the educators giving lectures, missing the opportunity to further empower students by having them present content. The important discovery that students creating content significantly increases their content knowledge (Bright et al., 2016) alerts us to the fact that this is an area of missed opportunity that future designs can leverage for increased student engagement and deeper learning.

To succeed in using CAO the educator needs to be a good manager, not just a good lecturer, which involves developing a completely different set of skills from those typically practiced by an educator (Leigh and Spindler, 2004). Cohen (1976) notes that "teachers have been hard-pressed to match leadership style to student needs to the classroom situation and to the concepts being taught" (p. 9). Rather than adopting one leadership style, CAO educators need to regularly flex their leadership style, sometimes enacting leadership that comes less naturally. Bright et al. (2012) elaborate on this idea by viewing CAO as an emerging system in which educators "facilitate and shape a class as a complex, adaptive, and living system" (p. 159). The role of both facilitator and manager in CAO is less about being in charge and more about supporting students as they make decisions and learn to become active agents in the organization (Leigh and Spindler, 2004; Leigh and Spindler, 2005; Bright and Turesky, 2010). As a facilitator of an emerging system, the educator needs to adjust the method of facilitating student activities in each phase as the organization matures and changes (Weil, 1988; Bright et al., 2012). Bright et al. (2012) discuss each stage of an emerging CAO and the particular facilitation that the educators need to enact at each stage (early, middle, and late) as the organization matures. It is evident that to teach CAO the educator needs to be prepared to be uncomfortable at times, and needs to be ready for personal and professional growth.

Element #5: Balance Structure and Ambiguity to Support Learning

The success of a CAO depends on finding the right balance between providing sufficient structure for the students while also incorporating enough ambiguity. Why ambiguity? Ambiguity creates situations in which students must become active agents – problem solving, making decisions, and influencing one another. Too much structure and the students are merely playing out a scripted game according to the educator's rules, resulting in a predictable but likely boring experience and surface learning. Too little structure and students become overwhelmed and learning becomes difficult.

In the CAO classroom, structures help students enact their roles, but are not intended to resolve all tensions. Bright et al. (2012) refer to the metaphor of a CAO classroom as a garden and the educator as the gardener:

> For instance, with some crops (e.g., peas or grapes), the gardener installs a trellis that shapes but does not determine the pattern of growth. On one trellis leaves form unique patterns each year. Similarly, the educator can set formal conditions for learning: the arrangement of the physical space, the enactment of class routines, and opportunities for student initiative. Students enact a classroom reality in response to these conditions. The educator provides a framework but cannot force students to learn. An initial class template becomes the trellis upon which learning grows (pp. 159–160).

Every CAO develops in unique ways even if you use the same structures. This is because students are empowered to make decisions and enact their roles and responsibilities as they see fit. The many decisions made by each student and each team throughout the semester produce a completely unique organization. This aspect of CAO makes it enjoyable for the students as well as for the educators; the emergent quality of the organization can be exhilarating and fascinating. There is a constant unfolding, a newness each time a class emerges into their own organization. In this way, the management abilities of educator and students alike are tested constantly as new and unique challenges unfold.

It is equally important to incorporate a certain amount of ambiguity into the CAO design. Ambiguity creates the need for students to make decisions and to take on an empowered role of shaping the organization.

CAO practitioners testify to the presence of ambiguity, the benefits of learning to work through ambiguous situations, and the tension that is created by ambiguity for both students and educators (Cohen, 1976; Bradford and Cohen, 1981; Balke, 1981; Sleeth and Brown, 1984; Lawrence, 1992; Meyer and Gent, 1998; Leigh, 2003; Lynn, 2010; Bright et al., 2012; Conklin, 2013). Emergent systems that make room for individual actors to shape organizational reality have a certain amount of ambiguity (Bright et al., 2012). Although educationally valuable, when faced with ambiguity students often become uncomfortable (e.g. Mezoff et al., 1979; Bright et al., 2012) and may push for more structure and less ambiguity. This tension tends to be strongest in the first weeks of a CAO and, if addressed properly by the educator, will most often transition into an enjoyable experience. The topic of ambiguity will be addressed in more detail in Chapters 3 and 4.

CONCLUSION

The CAO methodology emerged at a time when behavioral science was becoming increasingly relevant to management education. The four seminal articles from this time demonstrate the influence of the teaching philosophy of educational constructivism. The CAO method assumes that learning is an active process where students leverage their own experience and construct knowledge rather than receiving it passively from an outside source. Many CAO designs leverage specific constructivist practices, including authentic learning, flipping the classroom, and learning by teaching. CAO creates authentic organizations for student learning; it places the responsibility to learn theory on the student in order to use class time for learning in this authentic organizational context; it encourages students to learn through both peer teaching and peer assessment. The result is deeper learning and an emphasis on skill development.

The original CAO designs set the stage for important distinctions within the literature: interdependent organization versus leadered group designs; externally versus internally focused designs. The diversity of designs found in the literature makes simple categories difficult to identify. The literature review offered here discusses the CAO designs in broad strokes, illuminating similarities and differences: students designing elements of the course; applying the CAO methodology to different content areas; splitting the class in half; and developmental elements of CAO designs. The granular view of each CAO design reveals interesting complexities in each design. Although this chapter has documented the published CAO designs, there are likely many other versions of CAO that have not been published, and there is a need for continued evolution of CAOs for various course topics and purposes. However, CAO offers a significant change to how we view learning and teaching, and offers a dynamic, effective way to bring true organizational learning into the classroom.

Building on the foundation of this chapter, the aim of the next chapter is to provide educators an understanding of the key elements they should consider when adopting CAO.

3. Considerations for use

Given the complexity of CAO designs, it is typical and recommended, for educators interested in adopting this approach for the first time to draw on an existing model from the literature. The benefit of this strategy includes the knowledge that someone has had success with that particular CAO design. For this reason, Chapter 2 reviewed many examples of CAO in the literature, and Chapter 4 will present another example based on the authors' experience. However, whether you are designing your own CAO or implementing an existing design from the literature, there are important considerations for educators. The first group of considerations address whether CAO is a good fit with the:

- Educator's teaching philosophy and competencies,
- Institutional context,
- Basic parameters of class size, student level, required or elective course, and mode of delivery, and
- Combination of cognitive and affective learning objectives in the course.

Once it is determined that CAO is a good it, another set of considerations related to specific design elements of the CAO:

- Organizational design,
- Team descriptions,
- Peer teaching,
- Peer assessment,
- Structures for assessing students, and
- Student end-of-semester evaluation.

In this chapter, each of these considerations are discussed in turn. The intention is to assist educators in understanding the inner workings of the CAO methodology and assessing its utility for a given course.

CONSIDERATION #1: FACILITATING A CAO

A critical consideration in adopting CAO concerns whether it aligns with an educator's teaching philosophy, the core beliefs that underpin an educator's approach to teaching and learning. CAO requires a fundamental shift from being the "the sage on the stage" to "a guide on the side." Specifically, this shift involves sharing power and co-learning with students.

In a traditional classroom, power is held by the educator, who decides what gets taught and assessed, when topics and assignments are scheduled, and how class time is utilized. From this perspective, teaching competence means producing consistent results from the position of content expert (French and Simpson, 1999). The mental model that teaching is the transmission of information will get in the way of creating experiences that can impact practice directly (Ghoshal, 2005; Pfeffer and Fong, 2002; Weimer, 2013). Typically, content experts have deep knowledge in a particular area and are predisposed to paying "too much attention to theory [and] separate disciplines" (Farashahi and Tajeddin, 2018, p. 132). The result is the belief that there isn't enough time to cover all the required material. In reality, content expertise can hinder learning because the "central directive role of the faculty member in the class discussions or exercises can dampen the active engagement of students" (Kosnik et al., 2013, p. 616). The consolidation of power and emphasis on content expertise precludes the deep learning that is possible when students and teachers discover truth together by "working at the edge between knowing and not-knowing" (French and Simpson, 1999, p. 216).

In a CAO classroom, educators share power with students in ways that are appropriate to their developmental level. Instead of delivering content presentations, CAO educators focus their attention on managing tensions that arise, encouraging students to take responsibility, and helping them to make meaning of their learning by asking them to articulate what they think and feel (Bright et al., 2012). An educator's innate desire to deliver content disempowers students and detracts from the more salient learning that is occurring: taking initiative, dealing with failure, building accountability to their peers, and influencing others (Cohen, 1976).

Adopting CAO requires educators to embrace the role of learner in two ways. First, there is the requisite learning curve involved in adopting a new teaching practice. Since it runs counter to traditional teaching methods, teaching CAO for the first time may cause a certain level of anxiety. It is important to acknowledge and manage that anxiety because it can seep through to the learners and create a self-fulfilling prophecy within the classroom. Educators adopt CAO because it is an authentic expression of their teaching philosophy. However, the reality is that the first time teaching CAO requires the educator to live in the tension between experiencing anxiety while trying to exude confidence for the sake of the students. To balance this tension, it is helpful to have a "thinking partner" to regularly debrief classroom experiences. This might be a colleague or mentor who understands and embraces experiential learning, or a seasoned CAO educator who can identify with the complexity you are managing. Keeping a journal of your CAO experiences is a helpful way to process the experience and reinforce why you are doing it, what you are learning, how valuable it is for the students, and how it is an authentic expression of your teaching philosophy.

The authors all had a difficult first semester with CAO and yet subsequently became firm believers in it. We all struggled with anxiety and worked hard at improving our empowerment, coaching, and facilitation skills while practicing restraint when we wanted to take control. The first time through is the hardest, and it's important to get some personal support. Is CAO a good fit for you personally? Are you ready to take that leap into immersive experiential learning? Discussing these questions with a colleague can help mitigate risk and enhance the rewards of using the CAO method.

The second way that educators need to embrace the role of a learner is that CAO requires them to adopt the stance of a co-learner with students, partnering in an emergent process (Bright et al., 2012). Collaborative teaching methodologies working at the learning edge can produce anxiety for educators because of the requirement to be open to what emerges in the classroom as a result of the students who are present (Chappell and Thomas, 2019; Ramsey and Fitzgibbons, 2005; Tyson and Taylor, 2000; Raab, 1997). In this way, CAO educators must remind themselves of their commitment to educational constructivism: teachable moments will emerge; there is value in learning to work in ambiguous contexts; students have more capacity than I, or they, know.

Kolb and Kolb's (2009) learning cycle offers insight into the educators' role of co-learner and the iterative growth experienced in a CAO classroom. Both the educator and their students will continuously cycle through Kolb's learning phases: having concrete experience in the class-room; reflectively observing these experiences; making abstract connections to theory from the experience and observation; and then actively experimenting to improve the concrete experience. Kolb's learning cycle is also a meta-process that educators go through as they implement, reflect upon, and revise their CAO classroom designs.

CONSIDERATION #2: INSTITUTIONAL CONTEXT

The institutional context is a critical consideration when adopting CAO. Educators need to prepare key stakeholders at the institution for what lies ahead. Ideally, this means that the department chair and the dean have a broad understanding of what CAO entails. Specifically, this means that they support the following assertions:

1. Authentic learning, flipping the classroom, peer teaching, and peer grading (assessment) can be leading-edge strategies for deepening learning.
2. Students may struggle in adapting to the increased responsibility at first, but with a consistent message from the institution they will rise to the level of the expectations that are held for them.
3. The standard student evaluation form may not adequately assess what students have experienced and learned.
4. The first few iterations of this model may require some modifications, and so this requires long-term commitment.

Again, the context of the institution matters, as evidenced in the experience of the authors. Tenured faculty, or those who have the social capital to experiment, may not find all of the steps outlined here necessary. Regardless of the context in which CAO is applied, it is important to ensure a broad base of support. Here we outline several steps educators can take to garner this support and navigate implementation issues.

The first step in building support is to speak with your department chair to assess their awareness and support of CAO. Start with an overview of what CAO is and the learning outcomes it can produce. This step is about "teaching" them about CAO, and so multiple small conversations may have greater impact than a single long one. It can be helpful to review: (1) the organizational structure of the CAO; (2) one of the assessment rubrics that students will use to provide peer feedback; (3) the grading structure; and (4) the student experience (i.e. the change curve) and how the chair, and your colleagues, can be supportive. If it is appropriate, you can extend this to your peers by explaining CAO at a department meeting.

The dean is another important stakeholder when adopting CAO. Again, start with an overview of what CAO is and why you are implementing this teaching methodology. Summarize the potential benefits to students, the major, and the program that will result from including more team-based and skills-based outcomes for students. There are two key outcomes of meeting with the dean: (1) convincing them of the ways CAO can benefit the program; (2) preparing them for student resistance, and (3) requesting support for more than a single semester trial of CAO.

All three of us introduced CAO at institutions that were largely utilizing traditional teaching methods:

- One of us, operating in a context with a strong practice of academic freedom, implemented CAO as a graduate student by simply advising their department chair of what they were doing.
- Another one of us, a pre-tenure academic with a challenging relationship with their dean, was counseled by their department to hold off. The next year they partnered with a more senior academic to introduce CAO in a staggered fashion. As a result, CAO is now the standard format for the institution's first-year required management course.
- Another of us implemented CAO pre-tenure in the second year of teaching. Because of the risk entailed, this author sought explicit support from the chair, dean, and provost before implementation. CAO is now embraced by the department as an effective teaching methodology that adds value to the management degree program.

It is important for all stakeholders, including the educator adopting CAO, to understand that students will find CAO challenging. In particular, they may struggle in the first half of the semester because CAO requires them to learn a new way of being in the classroom (Chappell and Thomas, 2019). Scott and Jaffe's (1988) change model (Figure 3.1) can be applied to the student experience of CAO. Before they embrace CAO, students will focus on how the course is different from a traditional course. Students will start in the stage of *denial* (e.g. "surely, we won't be expected to teach and assess each other"); they will move to *resistance* when they start to be held accountable (e.g. "this isn't fair, appropriate or doable"), then to *exploration* ("maybe I could try to....") and, ultimately, in the second half of the semester, to *commitment* (e.g. "all courses should be taught this way").

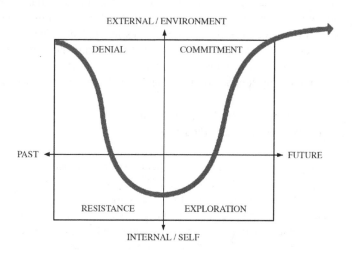

Source: Scott and Jaffe (1988)

Figure 3.1   Life cycle of student experience of CAO

Student resistance is quite predictable and, anecdotally, appears to lessen as the educator gains more confidence with the CAO methodology. Chapter 4 explores the life cycle in Figure 3.1 in more detail, including how the role of the educator changes in the different phases. Here, the intention is to highlight that it is possible that student concerns surfacing at the resistance stage may reach the dean or chair's office. Preparing them to respond to these concerns will inoculate their potential to derail your CAO. You might even prepare some language for what the dean, and your department chair, might say in response to each of these concerns, as outlined in Table 3.1.

It is also important to discuss the need for a longer commitment to CAO, one that extends beyond a single semester. The general rule of thumb is that it takes at least three iterations of teaching a new course preparation before the educator has a reasonable handle on the content

Table 3.1   *Sample script for dealing with student resistance*

A student might say	Possible response
My educator is not teaching me.	Professor/Dr. _____ has put a significant amount of effort into designing this cutting-edge simulation. This is based on the idea of the flipped classroom and authentic learning. There is teaching happening; it's just not in the format that you might be used to. I encourage you to observe your response to this new type of learning. I also encourage you to speak with Professor/Dr. _____ .
I don't know what I'm supposed to do.	I understand that there is detailed information in the _____. Have you consulted that? Also, is there someone in your organization (class) that might be able to help you?
I'm paying good money for an expert to tell me what is important.	This course is preparing you in many important ways to be an active member of an organization. You have access to Professor/Dr. _____ as an expert to consult on any of the aspects of the course that you are struggling with. If the answer is available to you in other parts of the organization/ class I know they will point you toward that in order to help the whole organization learn from your question.
I prefer working on my own to get work done.	This course is preparing you to work with and through people, which is what will be expected of you in the world of work. However, I understand how challenging this can be, particularly since it is so different from traditional classes. Stick with it; you might surprise yourself with how good you are at the process once you learn how to do it.

and design. This is particularly true with CAO because the learning curve is more ontological, and therefore more challenging, than learning new content. You are learning how to coach and facilitate student learning through a crucible experience. Again, the context of your institution will determine what is appropriate here.

The amount of work involved in gaining support for CAO will depend on the degree to which your department and/or institution are familiar with and embrace authentic learning, flipping the classroom, peer teaching, and peer grading. If these are well understood, the path to implementing CAO should be straightforward. If the institution is deeply entrenched in traditional teaching, it may be wise to invest some time (at least a full semester) to engage these stakeholders in discussing the above and educating them about CAO.

CONSIDERATION #3: BASIC PARAMETERS

While the principles of CAO can be adapted and applied to a wide range of classrooms, there are some considerations regarding class size, level of student, required or optional course designation, and mode of teaching, that need to be addressed beforehand.

Class Size

Class size is flexible in a CAO since the educator controls the number of teams necessary, as well as the complexity and difficulty of the team tasks, to create a functioning organization. The key consideration is that the class size needs to facilitate organizational dynamics. Cotton (1975) operated his organization with 30 students, while Cohen (1976) and Clare (1976) had more than 50 students. Clare suggested that fewer than 50 students would not produce the organizational complexities necessary for learning. The XB model (Putzel, 1992) has 16 unique roles in the organization, and therefore suggests no fewer than 16 students, while more than 30 are preferable. In fact, it is possible to run a CAO with a smaller class, although once the numbers become too low to reasonably create more than one team, students would experience team-level rather than organizational-level dynamics.

The authors have utilized CAO successfully in class sizes of 10–50, with the ideal being somewhere in the middle of that number. One of the authors has taught with only ten students in the CAO and reduced to three teams, making sure that all critical organizational activities are assigned to one of those teams. As the semester progressed the additional responsibilities were introduced and the students decided how to integrate those functions into the organization.

In order to recreate organizational-level dynamics, the ideal number is somewhere between 20 and 30 students organized in 5–6 teams. This class size creates enough complexity to challenge students to organize their work and find ways to influence the organization. Keeping the team size between three and five members ensures that team-level dynamics are present. It is possible to alter the team size or the organizational structure to accommodate the number of students. That said, with larger student teams (more than four per team) there needs to be enough responsibility built into the team descriptions to avoid social loafing. With more than 30 students in a class, the recommendation would be to create another team, with an additional set of tasks and responsibilities.

Course Level

CAO is not restricted to a specific level of student and has been used to teach undergraduates with little organizational experience (see Bradford and LeDuc, 1975; Cotton, 1975; Nath, 1975; Cohen, 1976; Clare, 1976), as well as MBA students (e.g. Bradford and LeDuc, 1975; Cohen, 1976; Pendse, 1984; Lawrence, 1992). However, depending on the level of the students, educators need to make adjustments to the course source material (i.e. textbook or readings) and the degree of structure provided. The purpose of teaching CAO to an undergraduate population is to create the organizational experiences to help them grasp and apply theory. In an MBA program, CAO assists in keeping the course content practical and applicable while integrating skill practice.

A consideration unique to undergraduate students is the different levels of structure and support required depending on their year of study (i.e. in a first-year versus a fourth-year CAO course), as both age and interest in the course subject positively influence a student's intrinsic motivation (Bye et al., 2007). Upper-level CAO courses are more likely to focus on a content area related to a student's major and so will, theoretically, be of more interest. In addition, upper-level students can draw on a greater range of experiences, including learning gained from their entire degree program. In contrast, first-year students will be dealing with the socio-emotional adjustment to a university context, and so will need more structure and support to be successful in a CAO.

The shallow and deep ends of a swimming pool provide a metaphor for the degree of structure in different CAO designs. The shallow end represents CAO designs with more structure, achieved through a combination of: detailed organization and team descriptions; an assigned reading package or textbook; limited peer assessment and teaching; explicit timelines for key events; established rubrics for all peer assessment, etc. Highly structured designs provide students with lots of support as they step into the CAO process. Students initially have limited responsibilities, and focus primarily on building strong relationships with teammates during the first weeks of the course. The educator provides active facilitation, clear and prescribed content, and suggested activities to get the students started. Student responsibilities gradually increase as their capacity to perform grows. The educator challenges students to work at the edge of their comfort zone to build confidence and skills before launching them into the deeper water.

In contrast, the deep end of the swimming pool represents CAO designs with less structure and more intentional ambiguity. This might include: greater inter-team interdependence built into team descriptions; increased peer assessment and teaching; delegating the choice of topics, assigned readings, and topic sequencing; increased responsibility for designing course policies and rubrics, etc. Students are expected to handle more responsibility and navigate greater ambiguity. Their responsibilities are defined, but they will need to develop their own processes and norms for fulfilling these responsibilities. Students have broad discretion and autonomy in how they do their work. This approach relies on the assumption that students have, or will develop, the requisite skills to successfully navigate these challenges. It also requires active coaching in the background on the part of the educator to provide perspective and support to students.

Is it better to start a CAO in the shallow or the deep end of the pool? This will depend on the learner's developmental readiness and underlying knowledge base. For example, the rubric for evaluating peer teaching would be handled differently in a shallow-end design (e.g. a first-year course) compared to a deep-end design (e.g. a fourth-year CAO). In both situations, the educator would provide the "structure" of facilitating a conversation on what makes a class engaging and valuable as opposed to boring and redundant. However, while fourth-year students could reasonably be delegated the responsibility to identify and collectively agree on interesting criteria for the rubric (i.e. no lectures, experiential learning, etc.), first-year students would find this challenging and would likely default to traditional criteria. Consequently, greater structure would be helpful for the first-year CAO; the educator might present a completed rubric, or a list of possible criteria for students to provide feedback on. Regardless of the structure in place, the role of the educator is to function as a "senior manager" and an active coach/consultant within and beyond the classroom.

Core or Elective Course

CAO can be successfully implemented in both core (i.e. required) and elective courses, although the designation is an important consideration. Elective courses have the advantage of students self-selecting the experience in response to the course description. In contrast, core courses do not have this advantage. Further, core courses often have multiple sections running in the same semester. If CAO is not implemented in all sections of a course offering, students in a CAO section will compare notes with their peers in a non-CAO section. There are two views on this. The first is that it is important to give students the option of different course designs to allow them to switch into a traditional course section if the CAO is not a good fit for their learning style. Another perspective is that allowing students to opt out may be a disservice given the applied learning opportunity that CAO represents: "a course is required presumably because the faculty believes that it contains core knowledge and/or skills, and therefore it is exactly for required courses that students should not be allowed to choose away from what the faculty has defined as essential" (Mezoff et al., 1981, p. 29).

The decision to implement CAO in a core course will likely require some discussion with your departmental peers, and the discussion below, on institutional considerations, will be particularly helpful.

Mode of Teaching

The published examples of CAO all occur in a face-to-face classroom. This is likely because the intention of CAO is to facilitate organizational dynamics that are often best resolved through face-to-face interaction. It could also be that the original versions of CAO were designed before the virtual/internet era. While there are no published examples of online CAO courses, it does seem that, given the right conditions, it could work. What are those conditions? First, the students would need to be at a developmental level to handle the lack of social support provided in face-to-face classes, that is, upper-level or graduate students rather than first- or second-year undergraduate students. Second, there would need to be specific structures in place to support real-time virtual meetings through video-conference systems (i.e. Zoom, Skype, etc.) rather than allowing fully asynchronous activity. This might prove challenging if students are operating in multiple time zones, but it is possible. Finally, it may be that some content is more aligned with online delivery. For example, a course on leading virtual teams might make more sense, while a course on interpersonal skills might not.

CONSIDERATION #4: LEARNING OBJECTIVES

Given the origins of CAO, one might assume that the method is only relevant for courses in organizational behavior (OB). However, CAO has been successfully employed in teaching policy (Balke, 1981), oral and written communication skills (Finan, 1992), high-commitment management (Lawrence, 1992), and can be modified for other business topics. Deciding whether CAO is appropriate for a course depends less on the content focus than on the learning objectives. A CAO approach is appropriate wherever an educator intends to have students apply content, practice skills related to that content, and develop reflexivity.

The specific learning outcomes of a particular CAO will vary depending on how the educator customizes and adapts the design. However, in principle the CAO methodology addresses both the cognitive and the affective domain in Bloom's Revised Taxonomy (Anderson and Krathwohl, 2000). As detailed in Table 3.2, cognitive domain learning objectives in a CAO course can range from *remembering* content through to *creating* with that content. These learning objectives would be adjusted depending on the level of the student, as discussed above.

CAO also supports learning objectives from the affective domain of Bloom's taxonomy as detailed in Table 3.2. Because of the intentionally built-in interdependence, CAO courses facilitate learning objectives such as:

- Demonstrate and practice leadership and influence skills.
- Practice giving and receiving feedback.
- Apply theory and course concepts to experience.
- Practice self-awareness and self-regulation.
- Practice being an effective organizational member.
- Discover and practice effective teaching methodologies.
- Expand their practical understanding of being a manager.
- Make decisions that result in expected and desirable outcomes.
- Engage and resolve complex challenges.
- Demonstrate and develop interpersonal skills.
- Synthesize learning from reflecting on action.
- Demonstrate commitment to excellence by going beyond the minimum.

Table 3.2   *Cognitive domain in Bloom's Revised Taxonomy*

Level in Taxonomy	Example of CAO Activities Relevant to this Domain	Key Words for Learning Objectives
Remembering: Recall previously learned information.	Students define concepts and theories through quizzes, in-class activities and/or exams.	Defines, describes, identifies, knows, labels, lists, matches, names, outlines, recalls, recognizes, reproduces, selects, states.
Understanding: Comprehending the meaning, translation, interpolation, and interpretation of instructions and problems. State a problem in one's own words.	Students identify examples of concepts and theories they observe occurring in the organization.	Comprehends, converts, defends, distinguishes, estimates, explains, extends, generalizes, gives an example, infers, interprets, paraphrases, predicts, rewrites, summarizes, translates.
Applying: Use a concept in a new situation or unprompted use of an abstraction. Applies what was learned in the classroom into novel situations in the workplace.	Students use concepts and theories to address issues they observe in the organization.	Applies, changes, computes, constructs, demonstrates, discovers, manipulates, modifies, operates, predicts, prepares, produces, relates, shows, solves, uses.
Analyzing: Separate material or concepts into component parts so that its organizational structure may be understood. Distinguishes between facts and inferences.	Students deconstruct individual-, team- and organizational-level behavior by applying concepts and theories during and after experiential activities.	Analyzes, breaks down, compares, contrasts, diagrams, deconstructs, differentiates, discriminates, distinguishes, identifies, illustrates, infers, outlines, relates, selects, separates.
Evaluating: Make judgments about the value of ideas or materials.	Students evaluate peer work related to application of content and theories.	Appraises, compares, concludes, contrasts, criticizes, critiques, defends, describes, discriminates, evaluates, explains, interprets, justifies, relates, summarizes, supports.

Level in Taxonomy	Example of CAO Activities Relevant to this Domain	Key Words for Learning Objectives
Creating: Build a structure or pattern from diverse elements. Put parts together to form a whole, with emphasis on creating a new meaning or structure.	Students develop learning tasks to address areas of substandard learning in the organization.	Categorizes, combines, compiles, composes, creates, devises, designs, explains, generates, modifies, organizes, plans, rearranges, reconstructs, relates, reorganizes, revises, rewrites, summarizes, tells, writes.

Source: Adapted from Anderson and Krathwohl (2000)

- Practice active listening.
- Distill priorities in ambiguous situations.
- Establish and maintain standards of performance.
- Demonstrate the ability to hold peers accountable.
- Demonstrate being proactive.
- Demonstrate reflective learning – Reflect on how they are using the knowledge.

The cognitive domain (Bloom et al., 1956) predominates in course learning objectives and program learning goals. For example, a learning objective that requires students to demonstrate knowledge of discipline concepts by identifying, explaining, and/or applying them to a theoretical case study predominantly requires cognitive competence. As detailed in Table 3.3, the affective domain (Bloom et al., 1956) concerns learning objectives ranging from *receiving and responding to phenomena* through to *internalizing values*. Failing to include learning objectives that address the affective domain results in a practice–theory gap (Bennis and O'Toole, 2005; David and David, 2011; Donovan, 2017) around the skills valued by employers, such as interpersonal skills, communicating clearly, motivating others, resolving conflict, and receiving feedback (i.e. Jones et al., 2017; Ritter et al., 2018). Creating educational activities that emphasize the development of such skills is possible, but rare (i.e. Ingols and Shapiro, 2014; Ritter et al., 2018). Since the cognitive learning objectives are relatively easier to assess, they tend to dominate educational activities.

In terms of Bloom's Revised Taxonomy, the decision to adopt CAO is appropriate when course learning objectives target the higher levels of

Table 3.3   *Affective domain in Bloom's Revised Taxonomy*

Level in Taxonomy	Example of CAO Activities Relevant to this Domain	Key Words for Learning Objectives
Receiving phenomena: Awareness, willingness to hear, selected attention.	Students ask for and actively listen to opinions and feedback from others.	Asks, chooses, describes, follows, gives, holds, identifies, locates, names, points to, selects, sits, erects, replies, uses.
Responding to phenomena: Active participation on the part of the learner. Attends and reacts to a particular phenomenon. Learning outcomes may emphasize compliance in responding, willingness to respond, or satisfaction in responding (motivation).	Students reflect upon and incorporate feedback from others regarding their output and their behavior. Students create strategies to solve problems, propose plans for improvement, and follow through with these plans.	Answers, assists, aids, complies, conforms, discusses, greets, helps, labels, performs, practices, presents, reads, recites, reports, selects, tells, writes.
Valuing: The worth or value a person attaches to a particular object, phenomenon, or behavior. This ranges from simple acceptance to the more complex state of commitment. Valuing is based on the internalization of a set of specified values, while clues to these values are expressed in the learner's overt behavior and are often identifiable.	Students initiate action in ambiguous contexts. Students demonstrate responsibility for outcomes that impact the organization. Students differentiate between priorities to meet the needs of the organization.	Completes, demonstrates, differentiates, explains, follows, forms, initiates, invites, joins, justifies, proposes, reads, reports, selects, shares, studies, works.
Organization: Organizes values into priorities by contrasting different values, resolving conflicts between them, and creating a unique value system. The emphasis is on comparing, relating, and synthesizing values.	Students compare intended outcomes with actual performance. Students synthesize relational values with operational efficiency in addressing conflict.	Adheres, alters, arranges, combines, compares, completes, defends, explains, formulates, generalizes, identifies, integrates, modifies, orders, organizes, prepares, relates, synthesizes.

Level in Taxonomy	Example of CAO Activities Relevant to this Domain	Key Words for Learning Objectives
Internalizing values (characterization): Has a value system that controls their behavior. The behavior is pervasive, consistent, predictable, and, most importantly, characteristic of the learner. Instructional objectives are concerned with the student's general patterns of adjustment (personal, social, emotional).	Students exercise influence. Students practice self-awareness and self-regulation.	Acts, discriminates, displays, influences, listens, modifies, performs, practices, proposes, qualifies, questions, revises, serves, solves, verifies.

the cognitive domain and/or the affective domain. In other words, CAO is appropriate when the learning outcomes transcend (but may include) content acquisition to enable students to learn how to put concepts into practice. CAO takes seriously the assumption that "learning by doing" helps students achieve an advanced level of mastery.

CONSIDERATION #5: ORGANIZATIONAL DESIGN

Organizational design is an important consideration, one that should be informed both by organization theory and the conceptual basis of the course. Organizational designs can range from hierarchical to flat, with many permutations in-between. The way the organization is structured will influence the kind of dynamics that emerge. The machine metaphor (Morgan, 1986) describes a hierarchical, bureaucratic system with levels of management and roles attached to power dynamics (Figure 3.2).

This organization design would be relevant in business courses where the practical application of the material is likely to occur in a hierarchical system, such as government organizations, divisional, departmental, or multi-national organizations. The value proposition for students in a CAO utilizing this organizational design is that they would learn to operate within a hierarchy, to accomplish and report assigned organizational tasks, and to monitor ongoing work. Working in a hierarchical organization, with the need to work across divisions, is good preparation for many first jobs after university. This type of CAO can also provide

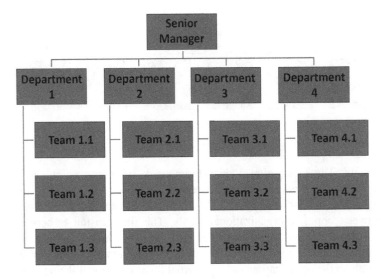

Figure 3.2   Organizational design for a hierarchical CAO

students the experience to effectively "speak truth to power." Both Cotton's (1975) and Putzel's (1992) CAO utilize the hierarchical organizational structure. However, there are potential challenges to the hierarchical model, as evidenced by Cotton's description of disempowered employees at the bottom of the hierarchy.

At the other extreme, the brain metaphor (Morgan, 1986) is reflected in a flatter organizational design, as depicted in Figure 3.3. This design facilitates multi-tasking and greater connectivity between parts of the organization. It would be relevant when the practical application of course concepts is likely to occur in organizations that emphasize collaboration, flexibility, resilience, and innovation. The value proposition for students experiencing this type of organization is the opportunity to create a humanistic culture, design meaningful work, and experiment with autonomy, responsibility, and recognition.

No one metaphor describes a single organization, and the metaphors discussed are just one framework of many that can inform the CAO organizational design. As important as the organizational structure is, there is more to organizational design than the meta-structure, and the organizational chart alone does not determine culture. Incorporating additional structures into the CAO design can influence how it will

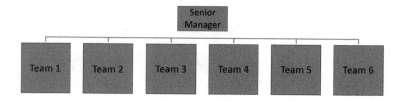

Figure 3.3   Organizational design for a flat CAO

operate. The Competing Values Framework (Cameron et al., 2014) is helpful in thinking about the relationship between structures and organizational culture (Figure 3.4). The framework names basic tensions between opposite organizational ideals. The first tension is between a flexible, innovative organization and one that holds stability and control. The second is between an internal focus on the well-being of the people in the organization and an external focus on the well-being of the organization itself.

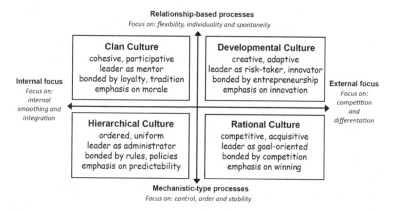

Figure 3.4   Competing values framework

The intersection of these two paradoxical tensions creates a four-quadrant framework of different organizational cultures: clan, developmental, hierarchical, and rational (Figure 3.4). For example, an internal focus and emphasis on flexibility will encourage a clan culture, one that is cohesive and participative, with the leader as mentor or coach. For the educator wanting to encourage any one of these cultures in their CAO, how can specific aspects of culture be built into the organization design? One answer lies in the important structure of team descriptions.

CONSIDERATION #6: ADDING STRUCTURE THROUGH TEAM DESCRIPTIONS

Team descriptions provide an important piece of structure in two ways: they articulate the team purpose in relation to the functioning of the organization as well as specific team responsibilities. As discussed in Chapter 2, effective team descriptions contain task interdependence between the teams and/or between a team and the whole organization. Unique descriptions for each team should contain some specific tasks, but also broad areas of responsibility with built-in ambiguity regarding how these tasks can be operationalized. For example, if the intention is to emphasize relationship-based processes, such as giving feedback, the team descriptions and tasks will make these explicit. This could be handled in two ways: assigning broad responsibility to a single team regarding the feedback process, or giving specific feedback tasks to multiple teams. Team descriptions should clearly articulate the "why" but leave the "how" as ambiguous as is reasonable, given the developmental readiness of the students. The descriptions need to be specific enough that students have a place to start, but not so specific that every task is explained in detail (sample descriptions are included in Chapter 4 and the appendices). It is the ambiguity that ignites the system's adaptive capacity by requiring students to interpret the meaning and take action.

The organizational theories outlined in the previous section, learning theories or theories relevant to the course content, can be used to create team descriptions. For example, the Putzel's (1992) XB model integrates a learning theory into the CAO by using the four stages in Kolb's learning cycle to name the four departments in his hierarchical organizational structure: Observing, Understanding, Doing, and Responsibility. Each department contains two sub-teams, each with specific responsibilities that relate to their departmental name. This theoretical overlay emphasizes an internal focus and relationship-based processes related to encouraging individual and group learning. For example, the Doing Department includes the *Directing Team*, which is tasked with facilitating the class meetings, and the *Communications Team*, which is tasked with managing organization-wide communications. By operationalizing

Kolb's learning cycle in the department and team structures, the XB CAO model influences the activities that occur and the resulting organizational dynamics that emerge. This theoretical overlay can be adapted depending on the content focus of the course (i.e. accounting, strategy, marketing, etc.).

Effective team descriptions provide the appropriate degree of structure. Too much structure suppresses student empowerment and the system's adaptive capacity. Too little structure makes the system chaotic, risks overwhelming students, and encourages low-performance norms. There is no exact formula for the correct balance between structure and ambiguity; rather, this is a function of different factors: the educator's comfort and skill with facilitating emerging systems, the developmental readiness of the students, the content and length of the course, etc.

CONSIDERATION #7: PEER TEACHING

The balance of structure versus adaptive capacity is particularly relevant to peer-teaching responsibilities in a CAO course. At the shallow end of the CAO pool the peer-teaching responsibilities outlined in the team description would be highly structured. This would include teams teaching a specific portion of an assigned textbook or reading set. Structure can be increased by: 1) specifying the order in which topics are covered; 2) assigning specific concepts/models/theories to each team; and 3) including conceptually based tasks in the relevant team description. At the deep end of the CAO pool the peer teaching responsibilities would be less structured. Rather than a textbook being prescribed by the educator, the task of selecting readings for specific content areas could be included in each team description. Quality control could be managed by specifying relevant criteria (e.g. one scholarly article, one popular article, one web page, etc.) and/or requiring approval of the readings by the senior manager before they are assigned to the organization. With regard to the content focus, rather than specific concepts being prescribed and scheduled by the educator, the task of selecting relevant concepts to accomplish a learning objective could be assigned to each team description. For example, a team description might include responsibility for teaching the organization members how to develop a marketing strategy. Students would need to research the topic and select the appropriate material to achieve the learning objective. Similarly, the task of deciding the order in which topics should be delivered could be added to a team description.

Regardless of how ambiguous or specific the assigned teaching responsibilities, students are encouraged to utilize experiential learning methodologies. In order for this to be successful, additional support from the educator is needed, including providing examples of experiential lessons on each topic. They will also need to meet regularly with each team to provide feedback to improve the lesson plans. Structure is also provided through explicit description of experiential teaching methodologies that are appropriate for their presentations and an explanation for why this teaching methodology is used. In addition, providing specific experiential resources for each topic assigned to a team provides the foundation for their success. For this reason, when choosing a textbook, it is important to consider whether it lends support to students for creating experiential activities around the topics they are assigned, such as self-assessments or supplementary resources that include experiential activities and debrief questions. Students may use these resources as they are, they may adapt them in interesting ways, or they may use them as exemplars for developing their own lessons. If a text is chosen that is void of any experiential activities, other sources need to be made available to the students, sources that the educator would normally use to find and create appropriate experiential activities on each topic.

CONSIDERATION #8: PEER ASSESSMENT

In contrast to a traditional classroom where the role of assessment and evaluation falls solely on the educator, CAO courses extend this responsibility to students. Delegating parts of the assessment can empower students in a real and meaningful way. The result is that students focus less on pleasing the educator and more on influencing and serving other class participants. Peer grading also provides an evaluation of work that more closely reflects the workplace. With the appropriate structures in place, students take this responsibility seriously and do an accurate job of describing the quality of their peers' work. However, there are multiple considerations related to peer assessment, including: the percentage of peer assessment to include in the assessment matrix; developing structures for peer assessment; ensuring high-performance norms; and adhering to student privacy policies.

The balance between peer- and educator-assessed components of the assessment matrix is an important consideration. The percentage of peer assessment needs to be significant enough to make it meaningful to students. Having some percentage of the grade determined by the senior manager encourages students to take into account the senior manager's expectations. At one extreme, peer assessment could be limited to a single element in the assessment matrix, such as the quality of peer teaching, or individual written work applying course content to classroom experiences. At the other extreme, 100 percent of the assessment matrix is peer assessed. In CAO classrooms, rubrics are critical. Course level does not determine the amount of the assessment that is peer graded, but it will impact the degree of structure required from the educator in the form of established rubrics. A related consideration is the amount of individual-versus team-level assessment, although this is not unique to CAO. The menu of options provided in the next section provides a selection of both.

Team descriptions should articulate specific responsibilities related to peer assessment. At the simplest level, teams would be responsible for assessing learning related to the concepts they are tasked with teaching. Team descriptions might require students to produce exam/quiz questions related to their content. At a higher level of ambiguity, the team description might require a strategy for assessing learning. Each team description can include one aspect of organizational work that will be assessed by that team (specific examples are provided in Chapter 4).

Without the appropriate structures in place, students will default to uncritical evaluation of their peers' work, resulting in artificially high grades. This renders the feedback meaningless and does not increase the quality of student work. One structure to combat this phenomenon is to utilize a forced ranking system, as in the XB design (Putzel, 1992), which requires students to decide whose work is best, second best, etc. Another approach is to require a certain amount of variance in grades (e.g. only 25 percent can receive a 90 or above, etc.). These structures encourage students to put forth their best effort, learn to articulate feedback (they have to verbally support their rankings to each other), and differentiate the grades. A negative aspect of these strategies is that when the whole group performs at a high standard, meaning all the work is excellent, students become unmotivated and the method becomes ineffective. Having some percentage of the grade determined by the senior manager can also mitigate grade inflation.

There is an important distinction between assigning a final grade and assessing individual pieces of work. Rather than asking students to provide a final grade for other students in the classroom, peer assessment requests that they evaluate the quality of students' work, contribute developmental feedback, and provide a *suggested* grade to the educator. The educator then assimilates all the suggested grades into a final grade and makes the decision about final grades. This is important in relation to the need to protect student privacy. Government regulations around student privacy (e.g. the Family Educational Rights and Privacy Act/ FERPA in the USA) can be incorrectly interpreted as a limit to using peer assessment. It is important to stress the fact that peer assessments are only grade *suggestions* and that the educator has the final decision on grades. The language used around peer evaluation is also important. Emphasizing from the beginning that these are suggested grades, and that the educator is responsible for the final grade, protects students' rights to privacy with their grades. The educator must stay vigilant, however, in protecting students' confidentiality in the grading process. One strategy might be to have each group keep a spreadsheet to compile their own suggested grades outside of the learning management system (LMS). Alternatively, if students have instructor access to the LMS, they could keep their suggested grades in the LMS and the educator keeps final grades in a separate location. Transparency and open conversations about the grading process throughout the course support the empowerment inherent in peer evaluation as well as the need for privacy of final grades.

Peer assessment is a powerful tool in the CAO context as it adds a layer of accountability and responsibility. Without it the educator risks giving students roles without power, which undermines the personal responsibility and empowerment that is possible. Ultimately the educator, and perhaps institutional policy, will decide how much grading power is put into the students' hands and how much is retained. A shallow-end CAO will have a lower percentage of student-recommended grading, whereas a deep-end version will put all grade recommendations into the hands of the students.

The authors have experimented with a grading system that is solely based on student-suggested grades as in the XB design (Putzel, 1992). We have also run a CAO where 60 percent of the final grade is based on peer assessment and 40 percent on educator grading. This decision is based on a combination of factors: the educator's preference; student developmental readiness; overall organizational design; and, of course, institutional expectations or constraints.

CONSIDERATION #9: STRUCTURES FOR ASSESSING STUDENTS

One important consideration in every CAO is finding ways to enforce a certain level of excellence in the course without taking back the power that has been delegated to the students. Whereas maintaining an emphasis on peer assessment is important, it is also important to establish standards for the acceptable quality and amount of work required to pass the course. By maintaining some assessment responsibility and assigning a significant grade percentage to this assessment, the educator retains the ability to enforce a standard of performance. In this way the educator prevents students from passing the course while free riding on the efforts of their team, and avoids forcing the students to make difficult decisions about not passing other students. The following is a menu of items that can be implemented in a CAO classroom as formative or summative assessment of student learning. The list includes specific mechanisms that encourage students to engage with material: Team-Based Learning, Chapter Presentations, Admission Tickets, Papers or Essays, and Journaling. In addition, a number of process-related mechanisms that encourage specific dynamics within the organization are included: Peer Feedback, Service, Participation, Attendance, Group Development, and Team Performance. Finally, a number of suggestions for the latter part of the course are included: Exams, Final Presentations, End-of-Term Self-Evaluation, and Exit Interviews. These activities can be peer assessed (P), educator assessed (E), or, depending on how the activity is formulated, both or either (P/E).

Team-Based Learning (E): Experiential learning is particularly effective when students have a basic understanding of the material *before* taking part in experiential activities. Team-Based Learning (TBL) (Michaelsen et al., 2004) involves quizzing students, both individually and in a group, on the material they have been assigned in order to assess their basic comprehension and readiness to engage with the concepts at a deeper level of application. The process of taking the quiz in a group reveals areas that require clarification. Integrating TBL into the CAO design models collaborative learning, influences how students show up for class, and encourages deeper engagement with the material after the quiz through experiential learning. Furthermore, TBL reinforces the flipped-classroom model employed by CAO through assigning weekly points to quizzes which are based on a mastery of the material before the class begins.

Chapter Presentations (P/E): One premise of CAO is that students master the material on a deep level by peer teaching. The assignment of course material should be included in the detailed task descriptions for each team. Student engagement is increased by peer-assessed chapter presentations, and it ensures that the presentations are relevant to the topic of the chapter and that learning occurred.

Admission Tickets (P/E): This requires the students to do preparatory work in order to encourage full participation in the class activities. As described by Balke (1981, p. 29):

> Each member is responsible for bringing to the meeting an abstract of a current article or actual experience relevant to the topic being discussed that day, along with an analysis connecting the organizational activities in the article to major concepts in the text chapter ... members without admission tickets are not likely to be called on during the day's discussions, and do not receive the points assigned for the tickets.

Papers or Essays (E): A paper or essay can be used to assess student writing, comprehension and/or personal growth. Writing prompts can be adapted to student developmental readiness and ability as well as course objectives. Adding a research component to the paper gives students the opportunity to delve into research outside of the textbook for a deeper understanding of academic literature on the topics in the course. These essays can be graded by the educator as a form of individual quality control.

Journaling (P/E): A weekly journaling assignment can be given to students. Creating journal entries, monitoring journals, and grading them can be student led. The purpose of the journal is for students to reflect on their own experiences and on the class topic. This helps students make the topics from the class real and grounded in their own personal experience. The act of reading and assessing peer journal entries reinforces and deepens this learning. Alternatively, journal entries can be graded by the educator to ensure quality reflection on the course topics.

Peer Feedback (P): Peer feedback is a powerful mechanism that can be leveraged in the CAO classroom both to create a virtuous cycle of continuous improvement and to teach students how to give and receive feedback. Peer feedback mechanisms can be created around individual student performance within their team, team-level performance in the organization, student presentations, etc. A meta-process of feedback on peer feedback can also be implemented. Giving a group of students the job of commenting on and improving the feedback students are giving one another strengthens the mechanism of feedback and emphasizes the students' role as they learn to give good feedback.

Service (P): To emphasize service to the organization, students can be required to create and implement a certain number of acts of service to improve the organization or assist members of the organization. These acts of service can be evaluated by a group of students and can become part of a student-suggested grade.

Participation (P): Typically, the educator decides on any participation grade given to students, but assigning this to organizational members adds a layer of creativity and engagement. Students need to find consistent ways to measure participation, communicate that to their peers, and provide feedback on the quality and amount of participation.

Attendance (P): Every CAO needs an attendance policy and attendance records. The educator can specify this policy in advance or ask the students to create it. Turning this responsibility over to the students is one more opportunity for student empowerment and involvement.

Group Development (P): One team can be assigned to measure group development in all the teams weekly. They will then report back to the organization the results of group development and offer training and group growth activities to help accelerate group development in areas of weakness.

Team Performance Grade (P): One team can help each team develop goals for their performance, measure teams against their goals, and provide developmental feedback to help teams become more effective at reaching their goals.

Exams (P/E): Exams can be included as part of the assessment strategy for all students, or can be used as an end-of-semester mechanism for students needing to improve their grades. Exams can be held inside or outside of class, through a paper or online format, at the individual or group level. Exams can be created by the educator, or teams can share the responsibility for writing exam questions.

Final Presentations (P/E): These presentations can be structured in a variety of ways. The basic premise is that students prepare and present professionally while demonstrating their mastery of the course topics by reflecting on the organizational history. Assessment can be by students or educators, or a combination of both.

End-of-Term Self-Grading (P): This is a final written assignment that asks students to assign themselves a final grade for the course and explain the basis for their assessment. If there is more than a letter grade variance from what the educator believes they deserve, a conference to discuss the discrepancy can be held. This helps students practice self-awareness and the skill of performance management.

Exit Interviews (E): During the last week of the course the educator can conduct exit interviews with each student to assist in their meaning-making regarding the CAO experience. Students can complete an exit interview assignment so that they have the opportunity to reflect upon their experience of the course in writing before the face-to-face interview. These interviews can reveal strengths and weaknesses of the course design as well as the depth of learning achieved.

This list is not exhaustive, but represents elements that you can choose to adopt in a CAO classroom, and recognizes that you may also choose to create your own elements. The CAO literature presented in Chapter 2 also provides a plethora of ideas for assessment elements that can be utilized in a CAO.

CONSIDERATION #10: STUDENT END-OF-SEMESTER EVALUATION

The consideration of end-of-semester student evaluation of teaching (SET), while related to the discussion on institutional support, is important enough to warrant a separate discussion. One of the benefits of the CAO approach is that collecting data from members of the organization (classroom) becomes standard practice. You can leverage this data collection process to demonstrate the impact of, and gain institutional support for, CAO. There are many ways to make this happen, but there are two specific strategies to begin with: 1) customizing the end-of-course SET; and 2) requiring students to submit an end-of-course reflection that forms the basis of an exit interview.

SET data is valuable in terms of continuous improvement (Spooren et al., 2013). However, SET data as a standardized measure of teaching effectiveness, particularly for tenure/promotion decisions, is contentious, with results of a recent meta-analysis suggesting that SET is unrelated to learning (Uttl et al., 2017). Standardized SET questionnaires are often designed with traditional teaching methods in mind. As CAO departs from the traditional classroom it is unlikely a standard form will adequately or fairly assess the student experience. How can students accurately assess a CAO educator who does not deliver content presentations by responding to statements such as "The educator was confident and

Table 3.4   *Sample questionnaire for CAO end-of-semester SET*

This course provided opportunities to demonstrate leadership.
This course enabled me to practice giving feedback.
This course enabled me to practice receiving feedback.
This course required me to apply concepts to experience.
This course challenged me to be proactive.
This course increased my self-awareness.
This course made me more aware of how to be an effective organizational member.
This course enabled me to influence the learning environment.
This course has expanded my understanding of being a manager.
The senior manager raised challenging observations that contributed to learning.
This course challenged me to do things I haven't done before.
Scale = 1-Strongly disagree, 2-Disagree, 3-Neutral, 4-Agree, 5-Strongly agree

competent with the subject matter" or "The educator made effective use of examples"? In addition, the nuances of the socio-emotional journey that students undertake in a CAO will not be adequately captured in a question such as "Is there anything else you want to say about the course?" CAO requires students to handle ambiguity and abandon the familiarity of didactic lectures. Consequently, SET evaluations that focus on student satisfaction will miss an important element of the learning that has occurred.

In some contexts, educators have the freedom to customize SET questionnaires by either designing their own or adding questions to a standard SET. Statements that might capture more of the story include "This course challenged me to do things I haven't done before" or "I learned how to provide/receive feedback on work" (Table 3.4). Additionally, end-of-course evaluations of CAO may occur too soon for students to make sense of the experience. Longitudinal SET evaluations (i.e. the next semester or the following year) may allow learning at an emotional domain to become consciously integrated.

Separate from the end-of-semester SET questionnaire, there are andragogical benefits to asking students to reflect on and make meaning of their experience. Given the opportunity, students will produce meta-cognitive insights about their behavior and learning that are both useful to their learning journey and powerfully persuasive regarding the value of the CAO approach. There are endless possibilities for how this might be structured, ranging from an open-ended response to a broad prompt, such as: "Reflecting on your experience in this CAO course, what have you learned about yourself, and how this material works in practice?" Alternatively, students could complete a structured question-naire (Table 3.5). Regardless of the design, we recommend making the reflection exercise separate from the course evaluation because they serve two distinct purposes.

Table 3.5   *Sample questionnaire for CAO end-of-semester reflection*

PART 1 (Multiple Choice):

Scale = 1-Strongly disagree, 2-Disagree, 3-Neutral, 4-Agree, 5-Strongly agree

1. This organization communicated very well inside the classroom.
2. This organization communicated very well outside of the classroom.
3. I am happy with the way [this organization] operated.
4. I am confident in my knowledge of the concepts taught in this course.
5. My team and I shared our work fairly.
6. This course taught me about how people behave in organizations.
7. My presentation skills have improved during [this course].
8. I was a good contributor to this organization.

PART 2 (Short Answer):

9. How do you feel about the way this course is organized? Explain.
10. Have your feelings about this course changed over the course of this semester? Explain.
11. What do you think [the organization] as a whole could have done better?
12. What do you think you could have done better?
13. Who do you believe was the most effective member(s) of [this organization]? Explain.
14. Which team do you believe was most effective? Explain.
15. What are two important lessons that you have learned this semester:

    a. About yourself? Why is this important?
    b. About working in teams? Why is this important?
    c. About how organizations work? Why is this important?

16. To what extent has [this organization] improved your ability in relation to each of the follow-ing (provide a specific example for each):

    a. Receive/give feedback?
    b. Take initiative in creating learning for yourself?
    c. Think critically and solve problems?

17. One definition of leadership is that "a leader is someone with the power to project light or dark onto an area." What is your definition of leadership?
18. In what ways have you grown as a leader over the course of this semester? What aspects do you still need to work on?

SUMMARY

In summary, this chapter explored key considerations when adopting CAO. The hope is that these are helpful for educators implementing an existing CAO model as it is, adapting a CAO to a specific context, or designing one from scratch. In order to determine whether CAO is appropriate, it makes sense to consider the basic parameters of class size, required or elective course, online versus face-to-face modality, and intended learning outcomes. Educators should also reflect on their teaching philosophy, institutional considerations, and whether end-of-semester evaluations might need to be adapted. Finally, there are important considerations regarding organizational design, team descriptions, peer teaching, and assessment structures. However, being intentional and carefully planning the CAO does not guarantee that it will unfold as intended.

Teaching CAO requires a willingness to be open to what emerges in the classroom as a result of the students who are present. The desire to produce deep and meaningful learning for students necessitates letting go of control and embracing a classroom situation that includes a range of emotions, from joy to anxiety, in order to achieve the aim of deep learning. The students will self-organize, act, and react within the structures designed, and there will be some unpredictable results. True to the nature of organizational culture, the CAO classroom is shaped by the actions of students who fill the organizational roles. Students will act in both creative and sometimes outstanding ways, and underperform in others. This is the adaptive capacity of the organizational system. No two CAO classrooms will be the same, even with the same structure and the same educator. You can set the guiding principles, but complexity resides in the people who carry out the organizational tasks as they react to their environment and one another. Sometimes the students will create an organizational element that works so well it becomes an integral part of the future CAOs, while other parts that fall flat will be modified or removed. It is important to approach CAO from a designer's perspective; it is a process of learning and adjusting as the tacit knowledge necessary to create and operate a CAO classroom develops.

Building on the foundation of the CAO literature base, this chapter explored key considerations for implementing an existing model or creating a new one. In the next chapter, a complete CAO course design is presented as a template for educators interested in adopting CAO.

Chapter 4 will map each of the considerations discussed in this chapter to a specific design.

4. How to prepare and implement a CAO course

Despite her expectation that she would encounter something different, Sam was surprised before she even opened the door to the upper-level undergraduate CAO class she was invited to observe. The low rumble of student voices, punctuated with sharp sounds from desks being rearranged, was spilling into the hallway. As the door closed behind her she looked for her colleague Maria, a master experiential teacher, who was teaching but was not at the front of the classroom. Instead, a small group of students was standing near the computer lectern, and music was playing: one was logging onto the online learning platform, another was writing an agenda on the whiteboard, and two others appeared to be negotiating revisions on a shared piece of paper. Sam was beginning to think she might have the wrong room because this looked more like a student meeting than an academic class. Before she could act on that hunch she was greeted by a friendly student who pointed her to the back of the room where Maria was sitting.

The music stopped and a voice from the front of the room shouted, "Ok OB Inc. it's time to get going." Slowly the noise dimmed and the students sat in their teams. The student continued:

> *We have a lot to do today. As you can see from the agenda on the board, we're starting off with a report from the teams that have collected data last week, then we're going to discuss our journal assessments, finally, we'll hand over to the Group Development and Growth Team who will be facilitating our learning more about motivation theory. Any comments or questions about our agenda?*

Members of the Team Performance and Feedback Team came to the front of the class and shared the metrics they had gathered from each team about their overall performance. They pointed out some great accomplishments and reviewed the difficulties that some of the teams were having. They asked the teams to discuss their upcoming goals and make a plan to address areas of underperformance.

Next, the Journaling Team put the rubric for assessing journal entries on the screen, explained the inconsistencies they had noticed regarding how students were assessing journal entries, and clarified the relevant points in the rubric. They gave the teams a few minutes to go back to the journal entries they had assessed and fix any errors. Sam leaned over a student's shoulder to see what this journal entry feedback looked like, and saw that the student was providing positive feedback on what she observed and areas for improvement as well as an overall assessment grade for the entry.

A different team asked everyone to direct their attention to the front of the room. They introduced themselves and outlined the agenda for their presentation:

MOTIVATION THEORY PRESENTATION

1. *Motivational video (3 min)*
2. *Teamwork (15 min)*
   a. *Define your assigned motivational theory*
   b. *Make up a skit to illustrate it*
3. *Perform skits and class discussion on motivation theories (20 min)*
4. *Brainstorm motivational systems for this organization*
5. *Voting and responsibilities*

The team moved smoothly through their presentation. While there were occasional stumbles, the class seemed highly engaged in the learning activities. Sam was surprised by the lively class discussions as the team debriefed the topic of motivation. The team had barely asked a question when students jumped in with their own questions, thoughts, comments, and examples. Maria pointed out that one of the teams was also actively and publicly tracking participation. Sam noticed that Maria also interjected a few times in the discussion to clarify a concept, and interacted with the teams.

At the end of the presentation, the Service Excellence Team asked the class what went well in the presentation. After a short conversation around three or four points, the team asked what they could improve. Another animated discussion ensued in which students praised the team and helped them with suggestions. The class was dismissed by the Service Excellence Team.

Sam was amazed by the energized and active learning environment. The students were engaged with course concepts, the materials, and with each other. What she observed confirmed Maria's assertion that students were gaining experience by creating the authentic dynamics of an organization where they influenced others, fulfilled responsibilities, and trained, evaluated, and engaged in meaningful organizational activities. Sam wondered, how did this happen? Was CAO an approach that she could learn?

INTRODUCTION

As an experienced educator, the dynamics Maria created in her classroom resulted from a commitment to the practice of experiential education. Inspired by the idea that she too can achieve this level of engagement, Sam has begun the journey toward becoming a different kind of educator. The intention of this book is to serve as a comprehensive resource for educators interested in adopting Classroom as Organization (CAO). The second chapter provided an overview of the historical context in which CAO emerged, the underpinning teaching philosophy and learning theories, and synthesized the CAO literature. From that, it is evident that each of the models of CAO arose out of the desire to create transformative, transferable learning through a course-wide, immersive experience for students. These original models of CAO demonstrate that it is possible to create an infinite variety of organizational dynamics, from ideal to highly dysfunctional. CAO provides an opportunity for educators to design organizations that allow students to practice the skills of acting and reacting in various organizational environments.

Building on this foundation, Chapter 3 explored specific considerations for implementing an existing model or creating a new one. These considerations highlight the complex process of understanding and creating CAO courses: each consideration can be operationalized in many ways, creating infinite possibilities for organizational structures within a CAO classroom. This chapter offers a complete CAO course design for an upper-level organizational behavior course, OB Inc., based on the authors' experience as they took into consideration the many choice points for creating a CAO.

All three authors found that the best way to teach CAO for the first time is to work with an existing model due to the complexity and wide variety of decision points possible. Each of the authors utilized the XB design (Putzel, 1992) as their guide to teaching their first CAO course. XB offered a template that helped build an awareness of CAO, aided in learning the facilitation skills needed, and provided a community of practice. Consequently, the purpose of the detailed course template of OB Inc. is to give a comprehensive example, along with the many others in the literature, of how a CAO can be put into practice. The intention is to offer educators new to CAO an option for their first CAO course. After completing a semester or two of teaching CAO, a return to the literature can provide an array of options to modify the structure or change aspects of the model to meet learning objectives. OB Inc. is informed by the body of CAO literature and our collective experience, as all three of us have taught variations of OB Inc. multiple times. While all the considerations from Chapter 3 are addressed in this OB Inc. design (as numbered in parentheses below), they are not necessarily addressed in the same order. Rather, the flow of this chapter is designed to clearly explain and orient the reader to the full organizational design.

A CAO is a complex adaptive system. While every effort is made in this chapter to describe OB Inc. in a clear and linear fashion, this is challenging. When one aspect of OB Inc. is described it is by nature integrally connected to all the other parts of the organization. Reading through the entire chapter will bring into focus the whole organization and its connectedness, while any section alone may leave unanswered questions about the organization.

OB INC.: A CAO EXEMPLAR

Basic Parameters (Consideration #3)

As presented in this chapter, OB Inc. is a face-to-face, undergraduate, organizational behavior course. The authors have implemented versions of OB Inc. in first -and fourth-year courses, and at the doctoral level. For the purpose of clarity, this chapter will describe OB Inc. as it was implemented in a fourth-year required course in which students had varying degrees of exposure to experiential learning. The course meets for roughly three hours a week (e.g., three 50-minute sessions, two 75-minutes sessions, or one 150-minute session) over 15 weeks. The syllabus can be found in Appendix 1 and offers details of the course. OB Inc. functions optimally with a class size of 10–30. The assumption is that students are in their final year, and have covered an extensive array of business topics as well as developed a variety of skills. For this reason, this version of OB Inc. will involve a higher level of ambiguity, student-led decision making, and extensive peer assessment. Since these students will soon graduate, one of the main purposes of the course is to ensure they gain practical skills that will help them successfully operate in an organization in their first job out of university. The text chosen for this course is *Organizational Behavior: A Skill-Building Approach* (Neck et al., 2018).

Institutional Context (Consideration #2)

As described in Chapter 3, each of the three authors has dealt with institutional considerations in different ways. Two of us gained support from our department chair and briefed the dean before implementing CAO. In addition, one of us gave an overview of CAO at a faculty meeting in advance of implementing CAO in the first year. This was reinforced a year later at another faculty meeting as the CAO method was extended to more sections. In the third year, the presentation (Box 4.1) included a handout with a sample of student feedback (Box 4.2) and a facilitated activity to demonstrate the type of feedback that students would experience. The data presented in Box 4.2 was curated specifically to illustrate the shift in student experience, from frustration with the ambiguity to eventual commitment to the empowering learning experience. The reality is that some students will exit the course with their commitment to lecture-based learning intact. For example, when asked if they liked the way the course was organized, one student said: "I personally am not a fan and would much rather be taught the normal way. That way being the professor teaching us the materials and us having to write notes." However, the dominant response from students is reflected in Box 4.2.

BOX 4.1   POWERPOINT PRESENTED AT FACULTY MEETING

CAO experiment:

- Year 1 = 2 sections
- Year 2 = 4 sections
- Year 3 = All sections (8 total)

Core philosophy: High-intensity experiential learning about DOING management.

Benefits:

- Higher engagement translates into greater retention.
- Students develop broader and deeper social networks.
- Students develop core interpersonal and managerial skills.

Challenges:

- Students bring a passive learning mental model.
- They will be pushed to the edge of their comfort zone – but we will support them.

What can you do?

- Expect students to complain about being confused.
- Reassure them that their feelings are part of the learning process.
- Encourage them to "stick with it," to "lean in by trying something – have a go."

Make the connection between discomfort and learning – and how their ability to navigate this course is something they will be able to talk with future employers about.

BOX 4.2 HANDOUT PROVIDED AT FACULTY MEETING

Have your feelings about this course changed over the semester? Explain.

- At the beginning, I could not wait for this course to end. I found myself overly frustrated and overly confused. I am so glad about how the course turned out and how hard I had to think and work to achieve my goals.

- At first I hated this whole organization thing. I was so used to having professors lecture, and memorizing things. This course made me work more and harder. It also made us make decisions and I wasn't used to it. But once the second [half of the course] hit, towards the end I began to like it.
- Looking back, I can appreciate what I have learned and can take away from this course.
- At the beginning of the course I was skeptical about the possible success and outcome, but now, having gone through it, I do like the change of perspective and feel great about the learning and leadership opportunity.

What are the two most important lessons that you have learned this semester?

- How to contribute to an organization; what it means to be part of a team.
- The most important lessons I learned are that everyone communicates in different ways and styles, and also that each person interprets information differently.
- How important communication is in an organization.
- The two most important lessons I learned were not to procrastinate, and to communicate effectively. Procrastinating too long will result in the work not being completed. Communicating is the only way to help the organization succeed.
- You must not take constructive criticism personally.
- That you can learn by doing and not by just having someone lecture at you.
- Getting things done does not necessarily mean they are done right.
- I have learned that I can be very influential and easily create relationships as I came into the semester a transfer student and will be concluding with many connections, as shown through the diagram showing trust in OB Inc.

Learning Objectives (Consideration #4)

The course catalogue description reads: "This course examines the complex and dynamic interactions of people and organizations in society.

Particular focus will be on organizational theory, human perception, motivation, group dynamics, power, conflict, culture, leadership, organizational development and managing change." The course objectives are for students to:

1. Identify and define key concepts and theories related to organizational behavior and leadership.
2. Apply key concepts and theories to examples from OB Inc. to analyze their experiences.
3. Critique and discriminate between applications of key concepts and theories.
4. Design structures and learning activities related to key concepts and theories.

In the process of meeting these cognitive domain learning objectives, the following affective, skill-based, and behavioral domain learning objectives mean that students will:

5. Receive and provide feedback.
6. Initiate action in ambiguous contexts.
7. Demonstrate responsibility for outcomes that impact the organization.
8. Compare intended outcomes with actual performance.
9. Practice exercising influence.
10. Practice self-awareness and self-regulation.

Table 4.1   OB Inc. assessment matrix

Assessment Component	Learning Objectives									
Quizzes individual	1									
Quizzes team	1									
Chapter presentations	1,	2,	3,	4,	5,	6,	7,	8,	9,	10
Service and participation/attendance		2,				6,	7,		9,	10
Team member feedback		2,			5,			8,	9,	10
Journaling grade	1,	2,		4,					9	
Group development grade		2,			5,	6,			9,	10
Team performance grade		2,			5,	6,	7,		9,	10
Personal application essays (2)	1,	2,	3							
Final presentation	1,	2,	3,		5,			8,	9,	10
End-of-semester self-reflection		2,	3,							10

The assessment matrix outlined in Table 4.1 demonstrates the relationships between the above learning outcomes and the course assessments. The details of these assessments are provided below in the section titled "Assessment in OB Inc."

Organizational Design (Consideration #5)

OB Inc. utilizes a flat structure of six teams reporting to a senior manager (the educator), as depicted in Figure 4.1. In OB Inc. teams are self-organizing; leaders are not specified, and everyone has equal access to the senior manager. A flat structure was chosen over a hierarchical one because this is consistent with the learning objectives. The flat structure, in combination with the team descriptions provided below, supports the emergence of authentic organizational dynamics and creates more opportunities for students to engage in leadership, influence others, and make decisions. Each person has an equal opportunity to influence both their team and the whole organization.

Figure 4.1   OB Inc. organizational structure

The names of the teams in OB Inc. reflect the course content, specifically OB and leadership. Successfully operationalizing the team descriptions requires students to practice skills related to the course topics. For each team, a detailed description includes the following:

• Team purpose: How this team contributes to and influences the larger organization. This specifically draws on the theoretical basis for the course: OB and leadership.
• Team tasks: These include tasks with varying levels of ambiguity. For example, some of the tasks are straightforward, such as arranging the room or taking attendance. Other tasks require an iterative process and/or consultation with other teams or the whole organization, such as creating a rubric to assess presentations.

- Teaching of content: Each team is assigned or chooses chapters that they will be responsible for teaching using experiential methods.

The organizational structure and the team descriptions reflect relationship-based values (versus mechanistic) from the Competing Values Framework (CVF), introduced in Chapter 3 (Cameron et al., 2014). In addition, OB Inc. emphasizes flexibility, individuality, spontaneity, and creativity. However, it emphasizes both internal and external values from the CVF. Internal values are reflected in team descriptions through tasks that require participative decision making and attention to organizational culture. The external values are reflected in the team descriptions through tasks that emphasize organizational innovation and improvement.

Team Descriptions (Consideration #6)

In OB Inc. the teams have differentiated and interdependent tasks; tasks are unique to each team and the impact of the task is organization-wide (Table 4.2). Each team's contribution makes a significant difference to the overall culture and has an effect on the organization as it reaches its mature state. When teams are high functioning and excelling at their tasks, the organization is doing well, whereas when teams falter the effects are felt across the organization.

Detailed team descriptions and tasks for OB Inc. are provided here. Each team will be assigned a team description and will embody their role in the organization throughout the semester. For the purpose of clarity, the term "team description" is used in this chapter and the related appendices. However, the term "team role" is likely more applicable during the CAO facilitation. While these are fully formed team descriptions for this particular CAO, when creating a new CAO new team descriptions can be created to fit the learning objectives of the course.

Culture and coordination team

This team enhances student learning by nurturing a culture and an environment that is conducive to student empowerment. This team helps everyone *be prepared* (understand what to expect for each upcoming class session), *stay on track* (adhere to the schedule for each day and for the course overall), and *coordinate* (stay informed and aligned relative to what others in the organization are doing). This team considers the routines and infrastructure that allow us to enjoy learning together at our

Table 4.2   *OB Inc. teams*

Culture and Coordination Team	This team draws attention to the course topic of organizational culture by instituting and maintaining cultural norms. They also coordinate the schedule and manage how time is spent in meetings (i.e. class).
Service Team	This team constantly reminds the class of organizational service by requiring regular service from each member of the organization.
Feedback Team	This team makes sure that regular, honest, helpful, face-to-face feedback happens. They also coordinate overall feedback and grading of chapters and final presentations.
Journaling Team	This team ensures that students reflect on phenomena that happen in organizational meetings and connect them to theory.
Group Development Team	This team highlights the team development process throughout the semester by monitoring the development of the groups using Tuckman's group development cycle and Lencioni's Five Dysfunctions of a Team.
Performance Team	This team holds organizational members accountable for fulfilling their team tasks. They create a system to measure and evaluate team performance regularly.

highest level. This team is successful to the extent that everyone in the organization knows what is happening when, feels empowered to proactively communicate across teams, and feels they have the time they need to accomplish their goals.

- Review Chapter 14: Organizations and Culture (Neck et al., 2018) early in the semester to gain a deeper understanding of culture; sign up to present this chapter for one of your presentations.
- Work with the senior manager and the organization to develop a schedule that includes sufficient time for assigned group tasks.
- Make sure that the room is arranged in an appropriate style, and that it is well maintained. Also, when each meeting concludes, ensure that it is left in a better condition than we found it.
- Compile and share with the organization a calendar of deadlines as well as a daily meeting agenda that includes all required tasks for this organization. Manage the agenda to keep the organization on schedule (or make adjustments as needed).

- Manage the meeting time. Designate a meeting facilitator to welcome everyone to the meeting, share the meeting agenda, host the meeting, and keep it on track according to the agenda.

Service team

This team enhances student learning by: (1) cultivating and reinforcing a culture in which students are mindful of and deliberate about their own and others' meeting participation; and (2) helping students pursue activities that will benefit the organization and their personal development. More specifically, this team is responsible for overseeing, evaluating, and providing supportive feedback on service records. This team is successful to the extent that each individual truly and fully participates in serving this organization.

- Train the organization in the process of gaining service points and utilize the service record sheet (Appendix 2) to facilitate students keeping track of their service.
- Review all service records at least once every three weeks. This should include giving feedback to each organizational member about their progress on service – tell them what their rating would be at their current level of progress.
- Provide organizational members with information on how you are evaluating their record according to the following criteria:
  - Variety: the member has accomplished tasks in several areas.
  - Time: the member has contributed to the organization both inside and outside the meetings.
  - Initiative: each recorded activity required initiative, courage, engagement, or thoughtful effort.
- Regularly speak to the organization about the value of service: share examples of specific creative service acts and give them ideas for service.
- Provide and maintain service sign-up sheets when needed (e.g. meeting observations, bringing snacks, etc.).
- *Provide the senior manager with recommended service and participation grades for each organization member at midterm and at the end of term.*

Feedback team

The Feedback Team is responsible for enhancing learning by helping organizational members to: (1) build safe and open communication climates within their teams; (2) hone their communication skills; and (3) provide teammates with substantive feedback. This team is successful to the extent that everyone learns to effectively communicate their needs and preferences to their teammates, responds positively to others' feedback, and proactively improves the viability of their teams over time.

- Implement a team member feedback process using the Team Member Feedback Form (Appendix 3). Make sure to include in the schedule at least three opportunities for this feedback process during the term: administer, compile, and discuss the results with the organization.
- Ensure that all written feedback is evaluated according to the criteria outlined on the team member feedback form.
- Provide organization members with regular suggestions about how to improve the quality of their feedback to teammates.
- Create and administer an organization communication system.
- Work with the organization and senior manager to create a rubric to evaluate team chapter presentations. Make sure everyone has access to and understands the rubric.
  - Use the rubric to evaluate all team presentations. This does not mean you need to complete the evaluations. You can ask people outside your team (e.g. get each organizational member who is not presenting to complete the rubric for each chapter presentation).
  - Lead a discussion after each presentation around the questions: What went well? and What could be improved? Provide teams with written feedback from this conversation.
- Use the provided rubric (on the learning management system/LMS) and organize the grading of final presentations.
- *Provide the senior manager with recommended chapter presentation grades for all organization members at midterm and end of term. Provide a compilation of the final presentation grades at the end of the semester.*

Journaling team

This group is responsible for enhancing learning by: (1) cultivating and reinforcing a culture in which students are carefully describing their experiences in the organization's journal; and (2) helping organization members be aware of how the organization has experienced the models and theories studied. More specifically, you are responsible for overseeing, evaluating, and providing supportive feedback on journal entries. Journaling is designed to help members develop their descriptive observation skills while creating a record of the organization's development. This committee is successful to the extent that the organization's history is meaningful, accurate, and interesting.

- Post weekly journaling topics to the organization on the LMS.
- Create a process to rate the quality of each member's participation in the weekly journal. You may choose to have all organizational members involved in the process of assessing journal entries. Utilize the following criteria:
    - Does their original post include a relevant theory from the text in the entry?
    - Does the original post make a personal application that is relevant to and illustrates the theory?
    - Is the original post interesting, compelling, and well written?
    - Did they make the required number of responses to other journal entries?
- Ensure that at the end of every meeting two people share their organizational observations – not general, obvious observations but specific things that happened that reflect on the topic of the week, or on topics previously covered. This is designed for us to observe and think about our organization in the context of the theories we are learning.
- *Provide the senior manager with recommended journaling grades for each organization member at midterm and end of the semester.*

Group development team (relationship)

This team enhances student learning by ensuring that each team receives feedback on their development as a team. More specifically, this team gathers data on how each team in the organization is progressing through the different stages of group development. This team is successful to the extent that all teams understand what they need to do to effectively navigate their way toward high performance.

- Review Chapter 7: Teams (Neck et al., 2018) early in the semester to gain a deeper understanding of group dynamics – sign up to present this chapter for one of your presentations.

- Teach Tuckman's Group Development Model (Tuckman and Jensen, 1977) early in the semester and have organization members identify the stage their team and the organization are at, as well as what could move them to the next stage.
- Check out this book from the library or purchase a copy for your team: Lencioni, P. (2005). *Overcoming the Five Dysfunctions of a Team: A Field Guide for Leaders, Managers, and Facilitators*. John Wiley & Sons.
- Facilitate a teambuilding activity from the Lencioni text weekly or bi-weekly to help teams develop and increase group effectiveness. Check the back of the book, which has specific activities for each section.
- Work with the senior manager to refine the Team Development Evaluation (Appendix 4).
- At least three times during the term, administer the Team Development Evaluation (i.e., gather, compile, and report on each team's development).

Performance team (task)
Your responsibility is to help each team be aware of their impact on the organization. You will do this through ensuring each team receives feedback on their team-related performance. If you are successful, each team will know how it is tracking as it works toward task-focused high performance. In specific terms, your job is to provide team-level performance information about how well each team delivers on its assigned task.

- Review Chapter 13: Influence, Power and Politics (Neck et al., 2018) early in the semester to gain a deeper understanding of performance management – sign up to present this chapter for one of your presentations. You will conduct the Power Simulation as your activity (http://www.leebolman.com/power_simulation.htm) for this chapter. Meet with the senior manager before running this simulation.
- Make sure attendance is taken for both weekly team meetings and whole-organization meetings (i.e. class sessions). Attendance needs to indicate excused and unexcused absences. Make this document publicly available.
- Create and maintain a filing system for the organization. Train members how to use the system. Everyone should have ready access

to any documents they need, as well as any assignments/forms they need to fill out.

- Work with the senior manager to refine the Team Performance Evaluation (Appendix 5) so that it reflects objective, team performance metrics.
- At least three times during the term, administer the Team Performance Evaluation (i.e., gather, compile, and report on each team's performance), including their performance on the goals they set.
- Hold teams accountable to the team contract they created in the first weeks of the semester (vision, norms, accountability).
- Make sure all teams write goals that align with their team tasks.
- Find ways to appropriately recognize those teams that are making a significant contribution to the organization.
- *Provide the senior manager with a recommended team performance grade for each team at midterm, and the end of the course.*

It's important to note that teams can be changed – either the team name and focus or the specific tasks of each team – to reflect the relevant course concepts.

Assessment (Considerations #8 and #9)

The assessment system built into OB Inc. (Table 4.3) balances both individual and teamwork, as well as peer- and educator-graded assignments. Details for each of these assessed activities can be found in the syllabus (Appendix 1), and a brief explanation is given here as well. Individual (60 percent) and teamwork (40 percent), peer-graded (60 percent) and educator-graded (40 percent) work are balanced (Table 4.4) as follows:

- Individual work includes: individual quiz grades, peer-recommended individual grades (service, feedback, journaling), and two personal application essays.
- Teamwork includes: group quizzes, chapter presentations, peer-recommended team grades (group development, team performance), and a final presentation.

Table 4.3   Assessment structure for OB Inc.

Quizzes individual	15%	Individual
Quizzes team	10%	Team
Chapter presentations *(recommended by Feedback Team)*	10%	Team
Service (5%) and participation/attendance (10%) *(recommended by Service Excellence Team)*	15%	Individual
Team member feedback *(recommended by Feedback Team)*	5%	Individual
Journaling grade *(recommended by Journaling Team)*	10%	Individual
Group development grade *(recommended by Group Development Team)*	5%	Team
Team performance grade *(recommended by Team Performance Team)*	5%	Team
Personal application essays (2)	15%	Individual
Final presentation *(recommended by Feedback Team)*	10%	Team
TOTAL	100%	

60% of your grade is individual and 40% comes from teamwork.
60% of your grade is recommended by peers and 40% by the senior manager.

- Peer-graded work, as noted in Table 4.3, is "recommended" by a specific team and includes: chapter presentations, service and attendance grade, feedback, journaling, group development, team performance, and final presentation.
- Educator-graded work includes: individual and team quizzes, and the two personal application essays.

*Table 4.4   Balance of individual/team and peer/educator
             assessment in OB Inc.*

	Individual (60%)	Team (40%)
Peer assessed *(60%)*	Service (5%) Participation/attendance (10%) Team member feedback (5%) Journaling (10%)	Chapter presentations (10%) Group development (5%) Team performance (5%) Final presentation (10%)
Educator assessed *(40%)*	Quizzes individual (15%) Personal application essays (2) (15%)	Quizzes team (10%)

Individual and group quizzes

For an experiential classroom to be successful, students need to engage with the subject matter before class (flipped classroom). For this reason, they are assigned to read and understand the chapter for the week before it is addressed in class. If they fail to do this, the learning in the experiential classroom is limited. The quizzes act as a mechanism to reinforce the importance of reading and comprehending the text before class, and are given enough weight to encourage students to take the reading seriously. The method utilized for the individual and team quizzes is an application of the Readiness Assurance Test (RAT) within the teaching methodology known as Team-Based Learning (TBL) (Michaelsen et al., 2004). In OB Inc. each quiz consists of 5–12 multiple-choice questions. The quiz is first taken by individuals, thus capturing their individual attainment of conceptual knowledge. When completed, the individual response sheets are collected, and then each team collaborates to take the quiz a second time together; collaboration is encouraged, but notes or other resources are not allowed.

While Michaelsen et. al. (2004) utilize a scratch card system for these quizzes, an effective and efficient method is to build the quizzes into the learning management platform. The individual quizzes are a straightforward setup, while the group quizzes include a "check" feature. Every time the team checks an answer that is wrong, one point (of three for each question) is subtracted. In this way grades are entered automatically and no paper or scratch cards are needed. This minimizes the amount of class time taken up by the quizzes, and maximizes the amount of time for the students to interact as an organization.

Peer Teaching (Consideration #7)

After the third week of the semester, students are responsible for teaching the course material in OB Inc. to leverage the deep learning that takes place when students teach one another (Putzel, 1992; Bright et al., 2016). Rather than presenting the information in the textbook chapter via a lecture format, organization members are instructed to make their presentations experiential through application-focused exercises (Box 4.3); this represents the second, and critical, element of TBL (Michaelsen et al., 2004). With six teams, each team presents two chapters a semester. Since the content in a CAO needs to follow the flow of team and organizational development, in OB Inc. the order in which content is presented is decided by the educator. In this way the content mirrors what organization members are experiencing at each point in the semester. Some chapters are assigned in team tasks so that content aligns with team roles. For example, the Culture and Coordination Team will present Chapter 14 on Organizations and Culture (Neck et al., 2018). Teams will choose from the remaining chapters which ones they want to teach. This happens in a class-wide negotiation process in the second or third week of the course, and will be described in detail below. For students to be successful at presenting chapter topics in an experiential way, they need support. Clear guidelines about the expectations for experiential activities that are related to the topic and how to lead a meaningful debrief are given in the syllabus (Appendix 1) as well as discussed in the first three weeks of the course.

BOX 4.3   CHAPTER PRESENTATIONS (EXPERIENTIAL LEARNING ACTIVITIES)

During each learning phase, your team will have an opportunity to create learning activities for others in the organization. You will help us master and/or apply concepts. The textbook (Neck et al., 2018) contains a number of learning activities which you need to review as a team and decide if you are going to use. You may decide to make up your own activity(ies). If you do, these need to adhere to the content of the chapter while helping the members of the organization actively engage with the content.

You must meet with the senior manager to discuss the activity before you present, and allow enough time to revise your plans if necessary. You will share accountability for the work of preparing and presenting. You need to think creatively about what can be done. Share media clips. Search on Google for games related to your chapter topic (i.e. "games for organizational structure") to see what you can find. The Management Teaching Review (https://journals.sagepub.com/home/mtr) and the *Journal of Management Education* (https://journals .sagepub.com/home/jme) have lots of articles on experiential activities for almost any topic in our course as well. You can also ask the senior manager for more resources and ideas for teaching. You will be evaluated on your presentations by a rubric that you as an organization will approve.

Examples of experiential activities for each chapter are provided in the text, and the senior manager posts alternative resources for various topics in the LMS. A critical requirement is for teams to meet with the senior manager before their presentations. During this meeting, they explain their presentation in detail and the senior manager helps them build a stronger experiential learning activity. At first students may struggle to accurately estimate the time needed for activities, or they may need help ensuring the activity effectively highlights the content of the chapter. They will also benefit from coaching on strong debrief questions. This is where the senior manager acts as an expert coach on the process of teaching; the process of asking questions and providing feedback helps the presentations become more effective. It's important to resist telling them what to do or how to do it. Rather, the emphasis is on pointing out the potential weaknesses and encouraging them to find solutions, thus preserving their sense of autonomy. Ultimately, the presentations are assessed by their peers, so they are motivated to ensure they are interactive and add educational value.

Suggested grades from teams
Four of the six teams have an assessment responsibility embedded in their team description as an explicit task:

- Service Team assesses members' organizational service based on service records.
- Feedback Team provides grades on (1) individual feedback for each member of the team, (2) chapter presentations, and (3) final presentations.
- Journaling Team provides assessment of the quality and timeliness of journal entries.
- Performance Team assesses overall team performance.

In order to produce the above grades, the responsible team will either assign grades or organize the process of all students providing input into the grade. For example, the Feedback Team provides a rubric for each member of the organization to assess the chapter presentations, and then they compile the results. The term "suggested grade" is used to avoid the notion that students are directly grading one another. The senior manager alone holds the responsibility of assigning final grades, as well as knowledge of final grades. With appropriate structures in place (i.e. rubrics and effective debriefs), members of the organization tend to provide a valid assessment of each other's work and engagement levels. However, ongoing conversations are needed to remind them that giving everyone high grades, as well as overly harsh grading, does not serve the organization or the learning outcomes of the organization.

Two personal application essays

The application essays (Box 4.4) are an opportunity for students to demonstrate their understanding of and ability to apply the concepts and theories presented in the course. The essays also provide an opportunity for students to demonstrate their writing and thinking ability.

BOX 4.4   PERSONAL APPLICATION ESSAY ASSIGNMENT

You will write two (2) individual personal application essays. You will discuss your own personal growth as a leader, follower, and functional contributing organizational member. You will use three major concepts from the text, explain the concepts – using one scholarly resource for each (you need three sources) – and apply them to specific observations of your behavior, experience, and personal growth in this course. The paper should be three to four pages long, double-spaced APA style with a cover page (no abstract). The structure is:

1. Introduction
2. Concept #1
    a. definition
    b. resource – description of scholarly resource and connection to your concept
    c. application
3. Concept #2
    a. definition
    b. resource – description of scholarly resource and connection to your concept
    c. application
4. Concept #3
    a. definition

b. resource – description of scholarly resource and connection to your concept
c. application
5. Conclusion
6. References

The process is outlined below:

- **Write a draft** and **post it** in the LMS by the deadline designated in the course schedule.
- Read your teammates' essays and **give them feedback** on their essay by the deadline designated in the course schedule.
- **Revise** your essay, drawing on the feedback you have received from teammates.
- Submit the **final draft** in the LMS by the deadline.

These essays are graded by the senior manager. By reserving some of the assessment for the senior manager, OB Inc. provides regular opportunities to gauge individual student work, as well as the opportunity to give specific and meaningful feedback.

Final presentation
The final presentation (Box 4.5) requires students to integrate knowledge from the course with their lived experience of OB Inc.

BOX 4.5   FINAL PRESENTATION ASSIGNMENT

The final exam in this course is a presentation that will require you to work with your team to demonstrate both mastery of course concepts and your ability as a presenter. As a team, you will perform an analysis of the history of this organization, using concepts that we have studied. The intention is to present your analysis as a holistic story using multiple presenters. Each member of the team should select one topic related to this analysis and prepare a 3–4-minute presentation. In total your team will have 15–20 minutes to present on exam day, with each person presenting on one topic, analyzing one aspect of the history of the organization for 3–4 minutes.

Teams present a historical analysis of the organization using theory from the course and illustrating it with events that happened throughout the course. The purpose is for students to explicitly connect theory to their organizational experience, cementing their learning. This project is graded by students using a rubric provided by the senior manager (Table 4.5).

Through the assessment and grading system, OB Inc. maintains the balance between individual and team grades, which encourages students to produce high-quality work individually as well as fully engage with their team. A high percentage of peer assessment emphasizes the power and responsibility members of the organization hold, and encourages students to meet their peers' standards and learning needs. Having 40 percent of the grade determined by the senior manager gives the educator space to reinforce quality standards and encourages students to take into account the senior manager's expectations as well as the expectations of organizational members.

While the above descriptions are helpful in understanding the individual elements of assessment, they do not provide insight into how the class starts, develops, or concludes. The next section describes how OB Inc. unfolds over the course of the semester in three distinct phases.

End-of-Semester Evaluation (Consideration #10)

The end-of-semester evaluation in OB Inc. occurs in two ways: through the addition of customized questions added to the standard institutional student evaluation of teaching (SET) questionnaire, and through an exit interview process (see Tables 3.4 and 3.5). One of the authors does not have the latitude to add or change questions to the institutional SET questionnaire, and so they have a brief discussion with the students about the evaluation form and some of the ways it does not adequately describe the teaching activities in OB Inc. For example, attention is drawn to the question "Did the professor explain concepts clearly?" The senior manager would facilitate a conversation around how to reframe the questions to suit the context of OB Inc.: "Although the senior manager didn't actually explain the concepts, did they create an environment in which these concepts were explained clearly?" In general, students are adept at recognizing the incongruences between the evaluation form and the course format and are able to adapt their responses appropriately.

The exit interview process begins with assigning the questions outlined in Table 3.5 as the final journal assignment. This is framed as the

Table 4.5 Rubric for final presentation assignment

Focus	Criteria	Points Awarded			
		50–46	**45–41**	**40–35**	**34–0**
Overall presentation for whole team	Flow/team integration	Logical flow. Well organized. Clear story of the organization. The pieces link together seamlessly and there was a sense that the whole team worked to make the presentation hang together	Some incidences with lack of logical flow. Some incidences where organization was lacking. Story of the organization was missing some pieces. For the most part the presentation was integrated between the presenters	Each presenter was well organized but there wasn't a sense of how the topics link together to form a story	Inadequate or illogical flow. Presentation lacked organization. The story of the organization was unclear or missing. The presenters seemed to have distinct presentations that were disjointed

Focus	Criteria	Points Awarded			
		10–9	**8–7**	**6–5**	**<5**
Team member #1	Delivery	Holds attention of entire audience with the use of direct eye contact, seldom looking at notes. Speaks with fluctuation in volume and inflection to maintain audience interest and emphasize key points	Consistent use of direct eye contact with audience, but still returns to notes. Speaks with satisfactory variation of volume and inflection	Displays minimal eye contact with audience while reading mostly from notes. Speaks in uneven volume with little or no inflection	Holds no eye contact with audience as entire report is read from notes. Speaks in low volume and/or monotonous tone, which causes audience to disengage

Content/ organization	Demonstrates full knowledge by answering all questions with explanations and elaboration Provides clear purpose and subject; pertinent examples, facts, and/or statistics; supports conclusions/ideas with evidence	Is at ease with expected answers to all questions, without elaboration Has somewhat clear purpose and subject; some examples, facts, and/or statistics that support the subject; includes some data or evidence that supports conclusions	Is uncomfortable with information and is able to answer only rudimentary questions Attempts to define purpose and subject; provides weak examples, facts, and/ or statistics, which do not adequately support the subject; includes very thin data or evidence	Does not have grasp of information and cannot answer questions about subject Does not clearly define subject and purpose; provides weak or no support of subject; gives insufficient support for ideas or conclusions
Enthusiasm/ audience awareness	Demonstrates strong enthusiasm about topic during entire presentation Significantly increases audience understanding and knowledge of topic; convinces audience to recognize the validity and importance of the subject	Shows some enthusiastic feelings about topic Raises audience understanding and awareness of most points	Shows little or mixed feelings about the topic being presented Raises audience understanding and knowledge of some points	Shows no interest in topic presented Fails to increase audience understanding or knowledge of topic
Team member #2	*Copy and paste from team member # 1 for as many team members as you need*			

Note: Calculate the total possible for each team (depending on how many team members) and divide the total score by total possible for a final grade out of 100.
Source: Adapted from Readwritethink.com Oral Presentation Rubric

preparation for a 20-minute one-on-one conversation with the senior manager. These conversations are extremely important for the students to meaningfully reflect on their experience. It is also an opportunity for the senior manager to provide individual feedback on what they observed: how the student engaged in the organization and the growth they demonstrated. This is a high-impact teaching intervention that varies depending on the student. Sometimes the conversation focuses on affirming and amplifying the student's self-reflection. Sometimes the conversation is geared toward gently challenging attribution errors related to the student's assessment of their success or failure in OB Inc. The interviews can take place during the last week of the semester and throughout the exam period. Although the exit interviews do require a significant time commitment, they are critical for leveraging student meaning-making about a complex and intense experience. The learning flows both ways in these conversations. Themes emerge over the course of the exit interviews that are valuable for fine-tuning the design of OB Inc. In addition, the senior manager gains insight into how and when they can do things differently; this is invaluable as the role of senior manager itself is a practice that is learned.

Facilitating a CAO (Consideration #1)

A CAO classroom is an emerging system, and the senior manager's role in creating a CAO is to "shape a class as a complex, adaptive and living system" (Bright et al., 2012, p. 158). There are three distinct phases in the process of shaping the CAO system – early, middle, and late – each of which informs the actions taken by the facilitator or senior manager (Bright et al., 2012). The role of senior manager is different in many ways from the traditional role of an educator. Even an experiential educator is at the center of the learning experience as they create and facilitate learning activities and debrief sessions. The power shift that happens in a CAO classroom requires the educator to embrace the role of manager, which depends on a different set of competencies. A senior manager needs to utilize the skills of co-learning, coaching, and facilitating. While the first few weeks of the CAO (the early phase) may utilize familiar facilitation skills, the middle and late phases shift power to the students and put the educator in the position of coach or empowering manager. The following explanation of each phase will highlight how the role and requisite skills of educators shift as the organization develops.

This meta-view of one semester-long cycle of OB Inc. will describe the flow of these three stages and how they relate to team development stages (Tuckman, 1965), and make explicit the transitions in the educator and student roles. In this description of the three phases of a CAO, Tuckman's group development stages are utilized to track where the organization is in its development and how the educator needs to accommodate the needs of students. According to Tuckman and Jensen (1977), all groups move through a predictable, if not linear, series of stages: forming, storming, norming, performing, adjourning. The forming stage begins when a team is established. Team members do not know each other well, are not sure about their task, and tend to rely heavily on the leader. In the storming stage team members begin their task and most energy is spent on relational matters; team members are vying for their place on the team and testing the boundaries of leadership. Storming is marked by relational and emotional struggles. During norming, group members build trust with one another and start making decisions together. Each member of the team is included and valued, and members respect the leader as well as taking on parts of the responsibility for leadership. In the performance stage teams become high functioning; relationships are strong, conflicts are resolved fairly quickly, and complex problems are solved together with relative ease. The adjourning stage marks the end of the team task, and the breaking up of the team.

In a course with 40 hours of contact time, the early phase represents approximately the first eight hours and includes the forming stage; the middle phase occupies approximately 16–20 hours, including storming and norming; and the late phase takes up the remaining time, including norming, performing (for some teams), and adjourning.

The early phase (8–10 hours)

This phase of the CAO focuses on building new norms and understanding between the educator and students, and sets the tone for the rest of the semester. This is the forming stage of group development (Tuckman, 1965), where participants are most interested in whether they belong and what this group has to offer them. Individual students do not yet fully understand the purpose of the organization, and so there is a sense of dependency on traditional classroom norms and the educator (Tuckman, 1965). In the CAO environment, students often feel anxious, confused, or excited at the prospect of a non-traditional, student-centered course. During this phase it is important for the educator to demonstrate confidence in the unfolding process of CAO and assure students. During this phase, as in a traditional class, the educator is in control of the classroom and leads the class sessions. However, they utilize class time to help students acclimate to a new structure rather than reinforcing the traditional classroom norms. This includes facilitating specific activities for students to get to know one another, to become comfortable with the unfamiliar structure of CAO, and to form teams. The broad objectives during this phase are to:

1. communicate and embed the rationale for this approach,
2. enable students to build relationships with each other, and
3. establish the foundational skills and processes necessary to be able to hand over the classroom to the students.

The intention of facilitation in the first three weeks of the course is to stimulate the conditions for emergent self-organizing. The goal of initiating a new organization necessitates that the educator takes a nurturing and supportive stance.

Specifically, the first three weeks of OB Inc. establishes the culture, introduces the structure, and orients the students to the organization. This stage is akin to onboarding new employees. An overview of the key deliverables for each week is outlined below and a detailed description of each activity is included in the appendices.

- Week One (Appendix 6)
  - *Email students before the first week to introduce yourself and advise them of the need to read Chapter 2 (Neck et al., 2018) and do a self-assessment online before class* (see Appendix 6 for ideas).
  - *Before class, arrange the chairs in a circle to indicate that this class is going to operate differently.*
  - **Icebreaker activity** – Starting the first class with this activity sets the tone that the class will be active and models the importance of experiential learning. It also helps students start learning each other's names, which is an important element of being successful in the course.
  - **First class discussion** – Lead students in a discussion focused on helping them to make observations and discuss them together. Move students beyond surface-level observations and facilitate a conversation about observations of the feelings and experiences happening.

- **Brief intro to the course** – Give a brief introduction of the subject and "why" of the course and the methodology used to teach the course.
- **Myers-Briggs Type Indicator (MBTI, or other self-assessment) activity** – Lead and debrief a self-assessment activity that builds a sense of belonging and appreciation of differences.
- **Create diverse teams** – Facilitate an activity to teach the difference between surface- and deep-level diversity, and identify the diversity present in the class. Facilitate the process of the students forming the most diverse and balanced teams possible.
- **Assign homework** – for students to decide on a time and place for their weekly team meeting, review the team roles and decide which one they want as a team, and review the chapters to be taught and decide which ones they want to teach.
- **Get volunteers** to lead "get-to-know-you" activities if you haven't already done so.
- Week Two (Appendix 7)
  - **Icebreaker activity** – One or two students lead an activity to enable students to become more comfortable with one another.
  - **Individual and group quiz** – Explain the process and administer the first set of quizzes on the syllabus and Chapter 2 of Neck et al. (2018).
  - **Team negotiation for roles** – Each team chooses their role in the class during a class-wide negotiation.
  - **Team negotiation for chapters** – Each team chooses the chapters they will teach during a class-wide negotiation.
  - **Discussion of teaching responsibilities** – This class-wide discussion will begin to set the expectations for what kinds of presentations will be most effective (experiential learning versus lectures).
  - **Tolerance of Ambiguity (ToA) exercise** – Students self-assess their ToA and discuss the importance of being able to expand their ability to deal with ambiguity for personal and professional reasons.
  - **Homework example** – Assign students individual and team homework (an example of a homework assignment is described in the Appreciative Inquiry Team Packet in Appendix 8). Students are also assigned Chapters 1 and 3 of (Neck et al. (2018).
- Week Three (Appendix 9)

- **Icebreaker activity** – One or two students lead an activity to help students to become more comfortable with one another.
- **Individual and group quiz** – Administer individual and group quizzes on Chapters 1 and 3 of Neck et al. (2018).
- **Appreciative Inquiry (AI) activity** – Students share the results of their team AI activities, which sets the tone for an appreciative way of functioning in their teams and as an organization.
- **Team time for getting organized** – Students have time to work in teams and/or as a whole class to get themselves organized for next week when they take over the organization.
- **Homework** – This week homework is not assigned; teams are beginning to self-organize around their team responsibilities.

After this initial stage of directive leadership from the educator there is a handover, a "go-live" date where the educator becomes the senior manager and empowers the organization; the rule of thumb is to hand over the classroom to students as quickly as possible. In OB Inc., week four is when the students are in charge. This handover signals the end of the early phase and marks the beginning of the middle phase.

The first three weeks are the only time you will be in charge of the class, leading from up front. By week four, when you turn the class responsibilities over to the students, your role, as well as theirs, shifts significantly.

The middle phase

In the middle phase (about 16–20 hours), when the senior manager hands over control of the classroom, students assume the roles assigned to them through the team descriptions presented earlier, and the senior manager assumes the role of observer/coach/manager at the back of the classroom. Collectively, the organizational structure and team descriptions function to delegate power and control from the senior manager to the functional organization, including: the specific topics to be learned over the semester, the assigned readings, facilitation of class meetings, and evaluation of student work. The storming and norming stages of group development (Tuckman and Jensen, 1977) become visible. Here students often struggle to operationalize the team descriptions and understand how to behave in a classroom that runs as an organization. For these reasons, chaos and ambiguity are the norm during this stage. Students are confronted with their own, and others', tolerance of ambiguity (TOA). They are required to make class-wide decisions in order to enact their team responsibilities in a meaningful and efficient manner. They are in the midst of creating rubrics and norms for the organization, all of which necessitate creativity, insight, and decision making. As this phase progresses, systems are being formed by students – some work well and some need adjusting or revamping after first attempts. Structural stability begins to emerge as the students establish routines and norms, entering the norming stage of group development. Students find positive and constructive feedback to be helpful as they take on leadership and influence the organization.

In the second and third phases of the course the educator's role morphs from facilitator to coach. Although the senior manager may request time on the agenda (5 or 10 minutes at the beginning or end of a meeting) to address the whole orgnization briefly, they will not be presenting content or taking control of class time. While the students take ownership of running the course, the senior manager's main source of influence comes through one-on-one conversations with individuals and meetings with groups, both inside and outside the classroom. During this phase the educator holds students accountable for outcomes, encourages students to authentically express their observations of the class, and encourages them to take risks, and to learn from mistakes. It is important that the senior manager does not encourage a dependent relationship during this phase by making decisions and/or offering direct answers to questions. Rather, it is necessary that students experience autonomy and responsibility within their roles.

When students make a decision that does not appear to meet an objective for the organization, the senior manager may struggle to let it run through to its natural conclusion. Rather than intervening by wresting control and redirecting the group, the senior manager should observe the group dynamics. Who is looking confused or potentially unhappy with the decision? The senior manager should approach them and ask them to reflect on their thinking and feeling, inquire about who they might share their thoughts with, and coach them on how to do so effectively. The student may or may not be effective in changing the course of the decision. However, when the whole class experiences and reflects on the consequences of this decision, powerful learning happens – much more powerful than when the senior manager makes the decision for the organization. The senior manager's role is to ask the students questions, helping them move through the process of making decisions on their own and taking action, not giving them answers or directing their efforts.

Students will be tempted to cut corners on learning. In an effort to deal with the ambiguity they will look for easy answers, satisficing in order to "make things work." The senior manager needs to find ways to hold the organization accountable by establishing norms that support the learning cycle. Again, this is best accomplished in one-on-one or small group conversations by asking questions such as: Are the goals of the organization (i.e. learning) being accomplished? How do you know this? Are students experiencing the positive dynamics of the organization? Are students providing helpful feedback? Are they holding one another accountable? Are they creating the results they hoped for?

One important aspect of the coaching role in OB Inc. happens through meetings between the senior manager and the teams intended to discuss and revise chapter presentations. While at the beginning of the semester much adjusting in the presentation is necessary, toward the end of the semester students become more adept at planning and presenting content through experiential learning modalities.

Another tactic to facilitate interaction with individuals and teams is using "team time" during organizational meetings; this is time that is designated for teams to work together. Team time is a perfect opportunity to discuss certain issues with teams. The senior manager can keep a list of questions that need to be addressed, and during team time can approach a specific team with a set of questions that will alert them to the issues they need to find solutions for. The ultimate goal is for organizational members to see what needs to be addressed in the organization and for them to raise these topics. Students also need constant reminders to take every opportunity for feedback and to make class-wide observations. When they observe what is happening in the class they should deepen their discussions about organizational behavior as well as their own understanding of the strengths and weaknesses of their organization.

The late phase
The late phase (the last 12–16 hours) of a CAO classroom includes the performing and adjourning stages of group development. During this phase students become adept at presenting content, discussing organizational phenomena, and relating concepts and theories to work and life experience. Students fully embody their assigned responsibilities in order to influence the organization and operationalize their team descriptions. The transformation is complete when their contribution creates a high-performing organization. During this phase students can push one another to ever higher levels of learning. It is equally common for students to want to reduce their effort here, staying in the norming stage where things are "good enough" and not pushing for excellence and

high performance. In this case the senior manager needs to be intentional about challenging them toward growth and to higher levels of learning. Even if the organization remains at the norming stage there is important learning in raising this issue and encouraging students to reflect on why this was the case.

There is no clear delineator to mark the beginning of this stage as there is between the early and middle stages. Some individuals and teams may reach this stage more quickly, pulling others along with them, while some teams may lag, struggling to effectively fill their roles. During this stage student relationships are deep and they are capable of giving and receiving honest and specific feedback from one another. Students are able to regularly debrief the classroom experience, helping each other reflect on their own growth as well as encouraging enthusiastic engagement in learning activities. It is also during this stage that the course will end, thus it is important to facilitate an adjourning stage where students can celebrate their success and appreciate their shared experience. The Culture and Coordination Team will facilitate a final class-wide discussion to assist students in articulating significant learning and bring closure to an intense, shared experience. In addition, an important part of the adjourning stage is requiring each student to conduct an end-of-semester evaluation.

CONCLUSION

This chapter has outlined one way to operationalize a CAO through the authors' co-created design of OB Inc. As described in the introduction, the intention of sharing this detailed description was to provide an exemplar for others to implement or adapt as appropriate to their context. It's important to remember that OB Inc. was designed to provide students with an experience of authentic organizational dynamics. Consequently, the principles of agency, connectedness, and feedback feature prominently in the design. OB Inc. intentionally encourages the capacity of students to act independently within the boundaries established by the course policies, organizational structure, and team descriptions. From the first day of class, OB Inc. emphasizes the need for students to engage and be present with others. Students realize they aren't going to sit in rows and listen to an educator; rather, they need the other students in the classroom to build a highly functioning organization. Finally, OB Inc. contains specific feedback mechanisms to foreground the constant flow of information that is available in the classroom.

There are so many ways to design and facilitate a CAO and this latitude makes it challenging to describe CAO. The OB Inc. design presented in this chapter represents a version that draws on the authors' experiences, but it cannot include all the possible adaptations without devolving into a confusing mess. Due to the incredible complexity of CAO, the best advice is to take a method from the literature and implement it as close to the design as possible, making the adaptations that are necessary in the given context (see Chapter 2 for discussion of context and the annotated bibliography in Chapter 5 for details of other CAO examples). After a few semesters you will either make bigger changes based on the considerations described in Chapter 3 or create your own. Along the way, remember the reason for implementing CAO in the first place: to create deep learning.

5. Annotated bibliography

The following articles represent the core scholarship on Classroom as Organization. CAO sits within the broader domain of experience-based learning. However, our decision criteria for this bibliography focused directly on CAO. For example, we have not included articles that mention CAO but are ultimately about a broader topic, such as experiential learning. The annotated bibliography is structured in chronological order from the first mention of CAO in the management literature.

1.   **Bradford, D., and LeDuc, R. (1975). One approach to the care and teaching of introductory organizational behavior.** *The Teaching of Organization Behavior,* **1(1), 18–24.**

Bradford and LeDuc describe a two-tiered design for using CAO to teach organizational behavior within an MBA program through an introductory course and an advanced course. In the introductory course the teacher randomly assigns each first-year student to a ten-person discussion group that meets for two hours per week. In the first five weeks of the semester the discussion groups are led through various activities to facilitate their group development. In the last ten weeks of the semester the discussion group undertakes a "major consulting project" which consists of diagnosing an existing organization structure, strengths, and weaknesses. Students in the advanced OB course are assigned to one of the discussion groups in the introductory course to act as group leaders. They facilitate exercises in the first five weeks, act as process consultants during the last ten weeks, and report back to their advanced class on challenges and progress throughout. This CAO design relies on the self-organizing dynamics of teams to teach team skills through an experiential process. The authors specify that the discussion groups are tasked with "remaining cognizant of their own group process throughout the ten weeks" (p. 22). Groups were asked to keep records of team behaviors, but specific structures were not described, either for tracking behaviors or for encouraging reflexive self-appraisal.

2.   **Cotton, C. (1975). When is reality not enough? The realism paradox in the simulation of a hierarchical organization: A major disaster.** *The Teaching of Organizational Behavior,* **1(4), 25–28.**

Cotton describes a whole-semester simulation with a class of 30 students, intended to provide an experience of "the internal workings of hierarchical organizations" (p. 25). Three layers of management oversaw the task of providing a resume distribution service through strict hierarchical communication channels. The professor, acting as the CEO, interviewed and hired three vice presidents, who in turn hired their teams through a resume review and interview process. Each week two-thirds of the class time was spent in the simulation and produced a range of organizational dynamics, which included: "poor communication and coordination, insufficiently trained and motivated subordinates, lack of delegation, procrastination, and the emergence, under pressure, of autocratic ... leadership styles" (p. 27). Student reactions varied according to their status in the organization, with upper-level management being quite satisfied and lower-level workers feeling alienated. Cotton concluded that "a technique which 'turns off' nearly two-thirds of the students [i.e. the 19 frontline workers] in a course is a major disaster" (p. 27). He proposes that a design based on the normative hierarchical organization contains a realism paradox: "if the simulation is realistic, lower participants become alienated and will not learn; if the simulation deviates sufficiently from reality to prevent this alienation, then all participants cannot learn from it about hierarchical reality" (p. 28). He suggests two possible solutions: (1) rotating people through levels of the hierarchy; and (2) changing the underlying values of the organization once the alienation of hierarchical structures is understood.

3.   **Cohen, A. R. (1976). Beyond simulation: Treating the classroom as an organization.** *The Teaching of Organizational Behavior,* **2(1), 13–19.**

This seminal article provides a strong argument for the unique benefits and key challenges of CAO. Cohen describes a design utilized with both undergraduate and MBA classes of 50 or more students. He describes the process used for creating heterogeneous teams, facilitating teams, self-selecting group leaders, developing team leaders, and utilizing job descriptions. Cohen recommends a reward structure (i.e. grading system) that includes both group and individual performance. The instructor assesses group-level work and group leaders are responsible for allocating this grade to the individuals within their team. Group leaders provide performance appraisals to each of their group members, which are in turn critiqued, in terms of their constructiveness, by recipients. Cohen describes variations in the structure intended to allow more students to gain experience in formal leadership positions. A keen insight is that faculty have often "moved to a somewhat more controlling managerial style than initially preferred" (p. 5) in an effort to work with the realities of a given context and meet students where they are at developmentally. Cohen stresses the importance of sequencing "course topics so that the material matches the students' in-class experience" (p. 5), which is thoughtful but also hints at an underlying assumption that the CAO format is only relevant for organizational behavior/development (OB/OD)-type classes. Finally, he offers his insight on the challenge of student resistance, the paradox of knowing when to intervene versus letting students resolve issues, and the need to be ready to hear students' feelings about your management style.

4.   **Clare, D. A. (1976). Organizational behavior, Inc.: Variation on a theme. *The Teaching of Organizational Behavior*, 2(3), 15–20.**

Clare articulates the advantages of the CAO approach for teaching the complexity of organizational dynamics. He contrasts his own CAO design, named Organization Behavior, Inc. (OBI), with Cotton (1975) and Cohen (1976). This design assumes a minimum class size of 50 split into divisions of ten students. Each division is led by a Representative and supported by a Historian and an Evaluator; the remaining members are assigned the role of Researcher. Clare recommends having "a standardized, predictable unit of work for those at the operative level in the organization" (p. 17), which in the case of OBI is a weekly report focused on how the topic of the week relates to the class. Clare provides brief descriptions of: (1) how he assigns members to divisions and to specific roles; (2) how Researcher reports are handled; (3) the Evaluator, Historian, and Representative roles; and (4) a grading structure in which each role is graded uniquely. As CEO, Clare's role is to "set the overall goals of OBI; establish the general agenda for achieving these goals; give lectures and set up experiential exercises; assist in case study analysis; evaluate the performance of the Representatives, Evaluators and

Historians; and work extensively with the Representatives both individually and in the Executive Committee" (p. 18). Clare makes an important case for allowing students to opt out: he suggests this can reduce some of the hostility that can surface when students are not expecting this type of instruction. Nonetheless, he finds it to be a successful teaching experience.

5. **Mezoff, R. M., Cohen, A. R., and Bradford, D. L. (1979). A dialogue on "treating the classroom as an organization". *Exchange: The Organizational Behavior Teaching Journal*, 4(1), 25–36.**

This seminal article connects teaching philosophy and pedagogical efficacy through a discussion between three early CAO adopters. Mezoff reflects on his experience implementing Cohen's (1976) model of CAO: student disorientation; dysfunctional group members; the change in power-distance; and alignment between CAO and certain learning styles. Bradford suggests the importance of using the principles "embedded in the content we teach as necessary determinants of our teaching method" (p. 28) and framing why CAO is being used: "The important learning in this classroom is to learn how to collaborate in work settings, to learn how to handle reward systems in which one's advancement is somewhat dependent on others, and to learn how to deal with problem people" (p. 28). Bradford asks whether students should be able to opt out of a CAO course (i.e. whether to use CAO in a required course). In response, Cohen proposes that allowing students to opt out of challenging learning experiences is a disservice. The exchange continues with keen insights from each author. One interesting point is the limited attention that Mezoff gives to orientating students due to "time pressures and because [he] is a very task oriented person" (p. 31). Mezoff also proposes a model for determining the appropriateness of innovative teaching approaches, which is not quietly critiqued by Cohen, who argues that "*not innovating* supports a loaded value system as much as *innovating* does" (p. 34). The final words come from Bradford, who reminds the group to think about the larger organization (i.e. the college, university, or institution) in which the classroom organization must operate.

6.   **Randolph, W. A., and Miles, R. H. (1979). The organization
       game: A behaviorally played simulation.** *Exchange: the
       Organizational Teaching Journal,* **4(2), 31–35.**

Randolph and Miles present an overview of their CAO design that
consists of four to seven simulations of 50–75 minutes that occur over
the course of a semester. The class is divided into four divisions that in
turn have both line and staff units. The divisions have minimal structure, and "participants must decide how to further develop and staff the
organization in order to achieve an effective system for the division and
coordination of work" (p. 32). Following each simulation, four objective
performance indicators are used to provide feedback to the divisions:
"scores on these indicators are affected by the productivity of the line
units, investments in organizational development programs, and events
such as member absences, dismissals, resignations, vacations, strikes and
underutilization" (p. 32). Each team is expected to leverage their experience and the feedback to become a learning organization that develops
its members. The article includes four graphs demonstrating decreased
task uncertainty and levels of differentiation, and increased levels of
integration and organizational performance. The actual simulations are
not included in the article but can be found in the book by Miles and
Miles (1979a). The Organization Game: A Simulation in Organizational
Behavior, Design, Change and Development. Scott Foresman & Co.
These simulations were used in undergraduate and graduate classrooms
as well as management training in the workplace.

7.   **Balke, W. M. (1981). The policy learning co-op: Treating
       the classroom as an organization.** *Exchange: The
       Organizational Behavior Teaching Journal,* **6(2), 27–33.**

Balke provides a detailed description of a CAO design implemented in
a senior-level undergraduate policy course. The course objectives are
for graduating seniors to: develop their ability to apply an integrated
set of policy concepts; develop career plans; experience a community
of inquiry; and develop their confidence to question and critique, to
act like managers. A unique feature in this author's design is the use of
class admission tickets, which encourage students to do research and
application in preparation for class. Balke describes course specifics such
as the organizational structure, individual and team roles, the format for
class meetings, individual and group tasks, the professor's tasks, and the

grading structure. In addition to task-related roles, "a number of positions are established so that each member can practice the variety of roles that managers take during meetings" (p. 28). Balke reflects on some of the problems he has encountered, including engaging passive students, procedural challenges, addressing performance issues, and the need for faculty support. Finally, he shares student feedback on the usefulness of different activities and the overall course. The detailed descriptions of each of the design elements in Balke's course make this a useful CAO model that can be adapted to different course topics.

8. **Bradford, D. L., and Cohen, A. R. (1981). Responding to student challenges.** *Exchange: The Organizational Behavior Teaching Journal,* **6(2), 20–26.**

This article provides helpful advice on how to handle students' negative reactions and anxiety about a class because of the way it challenges them (e.g., their social interactions, assumptions and norms, etc.). The authors explain that critical incidents are common in experiential OB courses, where students either refuse to fully participate or outright challenge the professor. They believe these incidences happen because of underlying anxiety, of both the students and professors, arising from the personally probing nature of OB classes. Professors' anxiety can transfer to the students and contribute to the classroom environment. The authors counsel professors to be ready for these incidents since the students are watching how the professor reacts to, and the outcome of, critical incidents that happen early in the semester. These incidents can set the tone for the remainder of the course. The professor who is feeling anxious may automatically interpret a student challenge as a personal attack, and may react in a way that breaks trust and creates an environment of hostility or disengagement. The authors' advice is to remember that students are likely challenging the professor out of their own personal fears and misgivings, and to deal with the challenge in a way that models the behaviors being taught in OB. Their specific advice to effectively deal with student challenges in a way that builds a learning climate is to focus (1) on the student's needs for support, (2) seeing factors that are interfering with student learning, and (3) using a spirit of inquiry (p. 26).

9.   **Obert, S. L. (1982). Teaching micro OD skills by developing
          the classroom organization.** *Exchange: The Organizational
          Behavior Teaching Journal,* **7(1), 23–26.**

This class design is focused on the application and practice of micro-level
organizational development (OD) and consulting skills. It has been primarily used for masters or doctoral students, but could be adapted to an
upper-level undergraduate course. Obert divides the classroom into two
groups. He creates competition, tension, and conflict between the two
groups as a way to teach them to deal with change, influence, power, and
other OD skills. The class starts with a four-meeting introductory phase
in which Obert frames himself as a consultant and the class as the client
organization and moves them through: (1) entry and contract negotiation,
(2) diagnosis, (3) force-field analysis, and (4) evaluation. In the second
phase students take part in a simulation in which both groups produce
political posters: one group has a hierarchical structure and the other
a self-managing structure. During the simulation, multiple environmental
issues are injected, creating a turbulent environment, after which teams
debrief their experiences. In the third phase each team writes a paper on
the simulation experience, gives their paper to the other group, and delivers a training session to improve the other group's skills. By this time,
tensions are running high between the groups and this activity results in
conflict. Students need to navigate the conflict as well as provide training
to a hostile group. Obert concludes the article with a summary of the
strengths and weaknesses of his course design.

10.   **Graf, L. A., and Couch, P. D. (1984). A program for
          managing student groups: An applied organizational
          behavior experience.** *Organizational Behavior Teaching
          Review,* **9(4), 34–40.**

Graf and Couch describe a two-tiered approach employed at Illinois State
University, an adaptation of Bradford and Leduc's (1975) MBA-level
CAO for undergraduate students. The first tier involves lower-level
management students enrolled in a basic management course in which
they attend "weekly lectures in classes of fifty or sixty, and then go to
a lab of fifteen to twenty people" (p. 35). The second tier consists of
upper-level students enrolled in a project supervision course, each of
whom is assigned the role of manager for one of the labs. They describe
how they train 20–30 senior-level leadership students each semester to be

managers of a team in another course. Students attend a weekly two-hour session to review lesson plans and exercises to be used, and to debrief the previous week. In addition, the authors describe the results of a survey of alumni. Survey respondents remember the course as valuable career preparation, and many felt the opportunity to perform the manager role was within the "top quarter of their undergraduate learning experiences" (p. 38). Despite the study's limitations, including the use of self-report data, it provides a good starting point for thinking through how one would research program-level results of this two-tiered approach, or any CAO.

11.   Pendse, S. (1984). *E pluribus unum*: Making a classroom an organization. *Organizational Behavior Teaching Review*, 9(4), 41–51.

Pendse describes specific structures to motivate group collaboration and collective productivity: having students measure group attendance and participation in proportion to the whole class, and providing student grades based on the data. He discusses the ways that a classroom does not resemble an organization and proposes ways to mitigate this. Pendse concludes that, for a classroom to become a full-fledged organization, "it is necessary that different groups play different roles in the work of the class, that some measure of their joint productivity be created and that their level of co-operation have an effect on their joint productivity" (p. 42). He stresses that there must be significant interdependence among class members and groups for a classroom to become an organization. Reflecting on a week-long team-bonding leadership training session he attended, he created some of these mechanisms and tried them in three separate classes. He organized the class to measure total attendance in the class and in the group proportionately, as well as the number of people speaking in class in each group. Students were graded on how their group fared against the rest of the class. Students gave reports on both attendance and participation, critiquing how the class was functioning as an organization based on this data. Pendse found that class discussions flowed more easily with higher participation and that attendance rates were higher as well.

12.   Oddou, G. R. (1987). Managing organizational realities: A classroom simulation. *Organizational Behavior Teaching Review*, **11(3), 72–85.**

Oddou describes a structured CAO that incorporates elements of manufacturing/production and markets, performance, and goals. He references Miles and Randolph's (1979a and b, 1984) design for a semester-long simulation and proposes an alternative developed for an introductory management course. Oddou groups students into companies that produce and sell integrated circuit boards. He explains how he divides the class into companies, how roles are assigned and rotated, and how company- and individual-level goals are identified. He also provides an overview of how class time is utilized and the general sequencing of the semester. In terms of assessment, Oddou utilizes a final exam worth 10 percent, a series of application activities worth 35 percent, a final group paper worth 35 percent, and individual peer performance reviews worth 20 percent. An interesting innovation in Oddou's design is the use of a weekly paper from the professor/CEO called *SimChron News*, which serves to communicate relevant market information that impacts student production decisions. Oddou suggests that the majority of faculty time is spent on grading small assignments in a "workbook," checking production quality and preparing the *SimChron* papers. Oddou concludes the article by contrasting his simulation with the one developed by Randolph and Miles and an evaluation of long-term simulations in general.

13.   Weil, J. L. (1988). Management experientially taught. *Organizational Behavior Teaching Review*, **12(3), 54–61.**

Weil shares his teaching philosophy and process for facilitating a class to design their own learning experience, including choosing content, making and implementing grading policy, running the classroom, and teaching each other. He describes this as a linear process of supporting students to answer three questions: (1) What do you want to do?; (2) Why do you want to do it?; and (3) How do you want to do it? He provides some examples of policies that the students have created for grading, attendance, and other requirements, such as "committee service, presentations, papers and role-play evaluations" (p. 59). Weil also explores some potentially challenging scenarios, including the possibility of a student refusing to sign the course agreement, disagreement over a peer-assigned grade, and peer assessments that are not critical enough.

In this CAO methodology a considerable amount of class time is spent on research, debate, and decision making, and the professor needs to be ready to work with the class through this lengthy and sometimes frustrating process while helping students assimilate the learning possibilities. All grades in this class are assigned by students as well. Weil does not mention the course content that he teaches in this format, but makes it clear that it would be appropriate for any upper-level management class.

14. **Gardner, W. L., and Larson, L. L. (1988). Practicing management in the classroom: Experience is the best teacher.** *Organizational Behavior Teaching Review*, **12(3), 12–23.**

Gardner and Larson describe a CAO design developed to address: (1) equity concerns regarding the selection of team members, non-performing team members, and peer grading; and (2) student attitudes and abilities in handling group work. The authors suggest that careful attention to managerial and team member selection (e.g., use of resumes, formal selection processes), performance appraisal (e.g., peer evaluation and evaluation of the manager's performance), and conflict resolution can mitigate these issues. For example, they describe three specific strategies for handling conflict: a detailed grievance procedure available to anyone in the organization; a means for managers to terminate a subordinate; and a process for team members to request a change in leadership. They suggest these are "typically not necessary, but when required are effective in resolving team conflicts" (p. 21). Finally, their design includes a Group Development Project (Schermerhorn et al., 1982) that requires each team to reflect, assess themselves, and plan for increased effectiveness on upcoming assignments. The authors conclude the article with a discussion of two specific challenges encountered in adopting the CAO methodology: adequately assigning students to managerial roles, and the different learning experience of students in managerial versus worker roles.

15. **Barry, D. (1990). Twincorp: Extensions of the classroom-as-organization model.** *Organizational Behavior Teaching Review*, **14(1), 1–15.**

Barry notes the weaknesses of CAO designs identified to date: the alienation of students in the lower levels of hierarchy; student disorientation;

failure to mirror critical aspects of organizational life; and lack of group interdependence. He designed a class on business policy to mitigate these weaknesses which includes small groups (Cohen, 1976), the consultancy approach (Tubbs, 1985), and the split halves organizational development (Obert, 1982; Steenberg and Gillette, 1984). Barry splits the students into two companies, or groups, with no assigned roles. The class time is divided into quarters: in the first quarter "company A" devises a strategy based on a case study and presents its findings, while "company B" is charged with observing "company A" in order to develop and implement an organizational strategy that will improve their performance. These roles are flipped for each quarter throughout the semester, with a new case introduced each time and other managerial constraints added. Barry's role is observer, taking copious notes and sharing his observations with the class during breaks. He finds this process central to student learning. He recommends a grading strategy of 60 percent for learning logs and 40 percent for presentations and feedback. Barry reflects on the normal cycles of the class, from confusion to failure to depression and eventually to high levels of learning, to help professors navigate the journey. He also explains ways to adapt the course design to organizational behavior as well as using material other than cases for the main body of the course.

16.   Miller, J. A. (1991). Experiencing management: A comprehensive, "hands-on" model for the introductory undergraduate management course. *Journal of Management Education*, 15(2), 151–169.

Miller presents a CAO where students design and run their own companies. The class meets two to three times a week for lecture sessions and twice a week in lab sessions. The class sessions are based on a management text and include lectures, discussion, tests, and papers; 50 percent of the course grade comes from these sessions. The lab sessions, where students create and run their own businesses, are initially taught by the professor but ultimately turned over to the teams. The labs include lectures/material on strategy and other topics relevant to starting a company. Students are given a manual to describe how the lab sessions are structured and what is required. Miller offers a timetable with topics for both sets of classes. Each company completes three independent projects: a campus or community service project; a business project (which produces profits to fund the service project); and a public report project. Class alumni in their third or fourth year can apply to be teaching assistants (TAs), who are integral to the success of the course. Progress updates are tracked in weekly "board meetings" with representatives from all companies, the professors, and the TAs. This class has been highly successful, one of the most popular in the university inside and outside the business department. Students report high levels of learning and lasting results from the course, although Miller reports that it is an "expensive" class to run as it requires exceptional amounts of time and energy. See entry #38 (Hendry et al., 2017) for an updated version of this method.

17.   **Finan, M. C. (1992). Manager and staff: A business communication course goes live!** *Journal of Management Education*, **16(4), 479–493.**

This article describes how Finan redesigned a traditionally taught communications course as a CAO course. She identifies the specific developmental opportunities her CAO design provides: individual skill in business writing, practice interviewing, and hiring; giving and receiving oral feedback in a group; giving and receiving peer critiques of written work; planning and presenting briefings and oral reports in groups, etc. The dual purpose of Finan's course was to focus on relevant organizational issues and create a sense of organizational membership in a class of first-year and senior students. Finan describes a course orientation carefully crafted to facilitate student interaction, which includes a cocktail party, a business card exchange, and two group-on-group facilitated discussions (Pfeiffer and Jones, 1974). She uses a matching process to create pairs of senior and first-year students where the former act as managers. These pairs collaborate to learn assigned content and also contribute as part of other teams (e.g., briefings, business presentations, providing feedback). An interesting design feature includes two renegotiation sessions to facilitate reflection and enable the organization to learn from experience. Finally, the process and focus of the self and peer evaluation, suggestions for improvement, and applications to other classes are discussed. Finan includes a very useful appendix of a course outline that details the learning objectives and key events for each phase in the semester.

18.   **Lawrence, A. T. (1992). Teaching high-commitment management the high-commitment way.** *Journal of Management Education*, **16(2), 163–180.**

Lawrence demonstrates how an instructor can create a CAO around a particular management theory. She describes the tenets of high-commitment management and how she implemented those principles in an MBA human resources (HR) class. Teams of 3–5 students are chosen and present case studies that run parallel to the course content. The first half of each class is spent in lecture and discussion. The second half consists of case presentations by student teams which are 50 percent graded by the instructor and 50 percent peer graded. Additional roles are assigned and rotated throughout the semester: critiquing presentations, organizing refreshments, and cleaning up after the class. Lawrence invites students to take ownership by bringing relevant news articles or current events to discuss in the first 15 minutes of class. Her design also provides multiple ways for students to be involved in goal setting and both self- and peer-appraisal. Lawrence finds that there are elements of the high-commitment workplace that are not replicable in the classroom setting and explains them in detail. She regularly discussed the parallels and dissimilarities between the class and high-commitment workplace with students, and had them write a final paper on the topic. She reflects on the shift in the role of a teacher in this setting, and suggests ways to empower students without abdicating leadership in the class. Overall, Lawrence found this to be a successful approach, but notes that there were many ways in which the high-commitment workplace could not be replicated in her CAO class.

19.   **Goltz, S. M. (1992). Practicing management in the classroom.** *Journal of Management Education*, **16(4), 444–460.**

Goltz outlines the value of designing a CAO with the goal of producing something that is relevant to students, in this case a campus survival guide. She makes three key contributions in this article. First, she succinctly describes three mechanisms for helping students connect their experiences to the course content: assignments, class discussions, and exams. Specific examples of assignments are provided to demonstrate how topics from a text can be directly applied to the CAO. Goltz discusses the importance of facilitating discussions that integrate class members' experiences with managerial concepts, particularly regarding the problems they encounter; and she suggests designing exams to "have students analyze class processes using managerial concepts and principles, as is done in class discussions" (p. 450). Second, she describes a CAO design in which the organization creates a product while dealing with real constraints, which makes the experience more realistic (i.e. equipment and budgetary control, product delivery deadlines, product quality management). Finally, Goltz shares a process for enabling all students to occupy the managerial role at some point over the semester. The typical sequence for a semester is described in detail, including the introductory period, the first three-week term, subsequent terms, the last class, and the final exam.

20. **Putzel, R. (1992). "Experience base" learning: A classroom-as-organization using delegated, rank-order grading. *Journal of Management Education*, 16(2), 204–219.**

Putzel provides a detailed description of a delegated rank order grading system, including the inherent benefits and costs. This article is extremely useful in providing the background to the author's CAO known as Experience Base (XB) Organization (Putzel, 2013). For example, how reading groups are integrated into the organizational structure is explained with a helpful diagram. The author's assessment strategy consists of 135 measurements of each person's performance during the semester, resulting in "so much data there is no doubt about how the person is doing" (p. 207). Students are required to use a rank ordering system to assess each other's work; within a sub-set of students, someone's work is deemed the best of the group, another piece of work is deemed second-best, and so on. The result is an order of students at the end of the semester where the instructor can see each student's rank and the overall distribution of rankings. Final grades for the course are determined by the instructor, who decides the break points and converts the accumulated ranks to letter grades. Putzel describes the benefits of delegating grading to the students, including the large number of data points, shifting the power base of the instructor from legitimate (i.e. grading) to expert, and forcing the instructor to specify what they are looking for. Additionally, he suggests rank ordering is critical to the success of delegated grading. However, rank ordering is controversial, and Putzel explores both the benefits and the costs.

**21.   O'Brien, C. D. A., and Buono, A. F. (1996). Creating
a networked, learning organization in the classroom.
Journal of Management Education, 20(3), 369–381.**

O'Brien and Buono share a CAO design for a flat and flexible organization that is based on networks of students who communicate vertically
and horizontally, allowing individuals to impact the whole system. They
outline an approach that is useful in "helping students begin to make a)
some of the necessary paradigm shifts required … as well as b) providing a sense of how horizontal processes can work" (p. 372). They share
a five-step process model that underpins the group development designed
into their CAO where students learn: (1) about the strengths, background,
and expertise of the other students in the class; (2) how to set working
norms and adhere to them; (3) how group and intergroup processes work
and how to make them more effective; (4) how to give and receive feedback on content, process, and performance issues; and (5) how to develop
self-knowledge. They share specific activities for addressing each of the
five group development processes in the classroom. The article concludes
with the author's reflection on the challenges of modeling a "networked,
learning organization" (p. 379).

**22.   Meyer, G. W., and Gent, M. J. (1998).
Organization-as-classroom approaches to management
education. In R. G. Milter, J. E. Stinson and W. H.
Gijslaers (eds), *Educational Innovation in Economics and
Business III* (pp. 99–113). Dordrecht: Springer.**

Meyer and Gent present a variation of Miller's (1991) design adapted to
a Principles of Management class (without the extra two days a week of
lab time). The first third of the semester is spent researching, debating,
and deciding on the business to generate revenue and the charitable
contribution that the team will make. The middle third of the semester is
devoted to making formal plans, policies, and procedures to operate the
business, culminating in a report given to a board that decides the amount
of capital the group gets. In the final third of the semester students revise
and implement the business plan. The final reports are prepared and
delivered, including a critical evaluation of the business process using
theories and principles covered in the course. Ultimately the authors
report that the experience of teaching this way was "hectic, frustrating,
contentious, confusing, and a major challenge for the students and for

us" (p. 103). However, they also observed deep learning that benefited students greatly in their further studies, interview performance, and future jobs. The authors note key differences in their context compared to Miller's that may be relevant: (1) support from the business sector; (2) contact time and credit hours for the course; (3) a 20-year legacy with archives of past business projects; and (4) the time advantage of students living on campus. The authors also review similar courses that have been offered at other universities.

23.   **Romme, A. G. L., and Putzel, R. (2003). Designing management education: Practice what you teach. *Simulation & Gaming*, 34(4), 512–530.**

Romme and Putzel provide an overview of the broad strokes of creating a CAO classroom, as well as providing specific examples of how these principles play out in classroom settings. The authors first explain five design-in-the-large (DIL) principles that guide the design of a CAO classroom, and then give two case study examples of classes that are being taught using the DIL principles. The five DIL principles discussed are: design the classroom as an authentic organization; utilization of peer mentoring and assessment; giving students both learning and management roles; professor delegation as a senior manager; and creating organizational and class structure to fit the desired learning. The two case studies include an undergraduate OB CAO design and a master's degree thesis writing circle created by Romme in which students take active roles as writers, co-supervisors (giving feedback on writing), and administrators.

24.   **Brown, R., and Murti, G. (2003). Student partners in instruction: Third level student participation in advanced business courses. *Journal of Education for Business*, 79(2), 85–89.**

Brown and Murti describe their experience of teaching an MBA class in which they leveraged self-directed and shared learning. They explain the process of listing possible components for the course, and through discussion and voting guide the students through a process of designing and building the class. The students agreed on grading and weights, and took on the teaching responsibilities. The authors give ten points of quantitative and qualitative data showing the success of the class, such as a 15 percent boost in overall attendance, a 36 percent boost in participation, a 6 percent boost in average grade, and the positive student comments about their own learning and enjoyment of the class.

25.   Leigh, E., and Spindler, L. (2004). Simulations and games as chaordic learning contexts. *Simulation & Gaming*, 35(1), 53–69.

Leigh and Spindler explore the relationship between chaos theory and human systems, suggesting that "a chaos theory framework can be of benefit in understanding and managing ... open simulations" (p. 54). The authors discuss three chaos theory concepts and then apply these to the facilitation of simulations. Using the XB model of CAO (Putzel, 1992) to explore these ideas, the authors offer clear suggestions for facilitators regarding the importance of initial conditions, strange attractors, and patterns. For example, they suggest that facilitators should understand "the value of attending carefully to the opening sequence of activity, creating good records of what occurs and being ready to use these appropriately when the need arises" (p. 63). Building on this idea, they suggest that facilitators "need to be alert to the earliest emergent signs of behaviors that may give rise to events that can affect positively or adversely" (p. 64).

26.   Leigh, E., and Spindler, L. (2005). Congruent facilitation of simulations and games. In R. Shiratori, K. Arai and F. Kato (eds), *Gaming, Simulations, and Society* (pp. 189–198). Tokyo: Springer.

Leigh and Spindler explore the importance of developing better facilitation skills for managing the learning process in complex simulations like CAO. The authors summarize and extend their exploration of how personal preferences of the facilitator influence the type of simulation chosen and the facilitation style employed within the simulation. They introduce the terms "moderator" and "improviser" to label two distinct "attitudes to the task of managing the learning" (p. 4) in a simulation. Their concern is that novice facilitators may "stretch closed [boundaried] simulations beyond their design parameters" or "limit the potential of open simulations by treating them as closed" (p. 5). Consequently, the authors draw on the theoretical lenses of learning styles and the Myers-Briggs Type Indicator (MBTI) to help facilitators design simulations to better align with both course learning outcomes and their own facilitation style/preferences.

27. **Putzel, R. (2006). Drawing on peer evaluation studies to manage the classroom.** *Journal of Business and Leadership: Research, Practice, and Teaching* **(2005–2012), 2(2), Article 13.**

Putzel reviews a number of broad themes related to peer evaluation: the historical evolution; distortions within organizational contexts; and increasing prevalence given to flattening organizational structures. He proposes that an important part of CAO design is to implement peer evaluation, which is both accurate and reinforces an important skill. Of particular interest is Putzel's discussion of the peer-evaluation structure he used in his 2007 XB CAO design: rank grading. He discusses how he overcame specific barriers, and provides qualitative evidence of rank grading in terms of contributing to learning.

28. **Putzel, R. (2007). XB: New paradigm management of the classroom as a complex organization.** *Journal of Business & Leadership: Research, Practice, and Teaching,* **3(1), 136–143.**

In this article Putzel proposes that even experiential activities can produce an environment in which students are not fully engaged. He introduces his CAO design, which he calls eXperiential Based (XB) and for which he has written a textbook that includes the operations manual for the organization. Putzel explains the basic tenets of CAO and then describes in detail how his CAO, XB, functions. He explains in turn the role of the senior manager, department (team) descriptions, and department tasks. The initial reaction of the students, as well as the process of how to lead through the development process in a CAO, is addressed. Putzel notes many benefits that he has observed from his years teaching XB, including that: organizational roles are real and have real impacts on the organization, and therefore produce practical learning; students become more engaged due to the conflict and underlying stress present in the mode of teaching; students practice leadership and influence; learning from failure happens regularly and is a powerful form of learning. Reference the manual itself (Putzel, 2013) for details beyond the article.

29.   Sheehan, B. J., McDonald, M. A., and Spence, K. K. (2009). Developing students' emotional competency using the classroom-as-organization approach. *Journal of Management Education*, 33(1), 77–98.

This article describes an application of CAO pedagogy in which students spend the semester planning and implementing a large-scale event such as a conference, large community service, or sports event. The major contributions of this article are the implementation of CAO to an event organizing class as well as quantitative data that shows student growth in emotional intelligence. This CAO course is designed around managing and marketing a basketball festival that is held on campus every year with over 500 teams competing; it has been running for 17 years at the time of writing. The course is an organization with functional departments: "tournament operations, volunteer management, marketing, sponsorship, registration, and finance and with the instructor serving as the chief executive officer (CEO)" (p. 82). Students participate in staff meetings, generate action items for the agenda, lead discussions, give departmental updates, solve problems, and make decisions. They write in a personal reflection journal to "actively participate in their personal and professional growth by thinking about and reflecting on their daily event management experiences over the course of the semester" (p. 85) as well as meeting one-on-one with the professor each month. The course wraps up with a final performance essay and an exit interview. The mixed method study results show that emotional intelligence competencies are improved in this CAO format significantly more than in a traditional teaching format.

30.   Bright, D. S., and Turesky, E. F. (2010). Fostering student-to-student feedback: A condition for emergent learning in the classroom. Paper presented at the Organizational Behavior Teaching Conference, Albuquerque, New Mexico.

This is a workshop proposal that was delivered at the Organizational Behavior Teaching Society (OBTS) annual conference and is a useful resource for educators interested in fostering engaged and helpful feedback between students. This paper succinctly describes the classroom as a living and emergent system. The authors focus on a specific condition that is necessary for this emergence: high-quality peer-to-peer feedback.

They describe two specific processes: peer feedback on personal application papers, and a performance management system for students to self-manage. Both processes are described in enough detail to support implementation by the reader. Relevant and comprehensive resources are included as appendices. Readers are encouraged to email David Bright (david.bright@wright.edu) for a copy of the paper if interested.

31. **Lynn, M. L. (2010). Venture Out: An entrepreneurial introduction to business.** *Christian Business Academy Review*, **5, 31–36.**

Lynn adapts Miller's (1991) design to a lower-level management class that only meets three times a week. In contrast to Meyer and Gent (1998), who emphasize the difficulties of their adaptation of Miller's design, Lynn does not allude to any particular difficulty in running the course. This course, which requires students to start and run a business during their Introduction to Business course, meets twice a week for coursework and once a week as a business. Like Miller's design, students apply for a loan, run a business, and donate the profits to a charity. There are various adaptations to this course. Students work in groups of eight instead of Miller's groups of 30. Mid-semester students present their plans to a board made up of professors and business professionals to qualify for a $500 loan that must be paid back by the end of the semester. The fact that this course has run successfully since 2010 shows that some of the same learning objectives that Miller gets from three regular class times and two long labs a week can happen within a traditional class schedule of three hours per week. Benefits to students are self-reported and the program encourages active engagement with the local business community.

32. **Hannah, D. R., and Venkatachary, R. (2010). Putting "organizations" into an organization theory course: A hybrid CAO model for teaching organization theory.** *Journal of Management Education*, **34(2), 200–223.**

The authors share a reflective analysis of the development and evolution of an undergraduate Organizational Theory course delivered eight times over six years. In the first half of the three-hour class the instructor delivered content. The second part of the class was reserved for students to work on application activities in organizations of 12–24 students. Each of the six organizations elected a CEO and two VPs who in turn managed subgroups of students. The authors use both qualitative (i.e. student comments) and quantitative (i.e. statistical analysis of student end-of-course surveys) data to illustrate the successes, challenges, and evolution of the course design. They suggest three critical features for CAO design to deliver effective learning: relevant material, authenticity of the design, and the physical space employed. They share specific strategies employed for increasing course relevance and authenticity. For example, to increase content relevance of the course the instructor moved away from generic case analysis to selecting application activities that were clearly and explicitly relevant to the lecture material. Another strategy was the introduction of assignments, at both organization and individual level, to facilitate application of course concepts. The authors conclude with some thoughts on managing student workload and a summary table listing the key phases in their 14-week course design.

33.   André, R. (2011). Using leadered groups in organizational behavior and management survey courses. *Journal of Management Education*, 35(5), 596–619.

André proposes a method for teaching leadership skills by implementing leadership rotation rather than utilizing the leaderless group design. She argues that it is critical that students in undergraduate management courses get to practice leadership skills, and therefore encourages professors to adopt a rotating leadered group model. The author notes that in leaderless groups each student falls into their "normal" role, whether that is the high achiever or the freeloader, and contends that rotating leadership stretches students to take on other roles, mitigating the problems that arise in leaderless groups. Design elements include: "the opportunity to lead, responsibility to lead well, accountability for leadership effectiveness and feedback on leadership technique" (p. 601). Eight class periods are devoted to the process: one for teaching the group process, one leaderless group project, and six devoted to leadered group projects. The class culminates with a final project in which students reflect on the group process throughout the semester, utilizing concepts from the class. The author gives samples of group projects that could be used in an OB course as well as a feedback form to be filled out by non-leading members at the conclusion of each project.

**34. McDonald, M., Spence, K., and Sheehan, B. (2011).
Classroom-as-organization: An integral approach.** *Journal
of Integral Theory and Practice,* **6(2), 67–81.**

McDonald, Spence, and Sheehan demonstrate how the CAO methodology can be applied to a sport-management or other event-planning
course. A key contribution of this article is understanding the developmental potential of CAO from an integral theory perspective. The article
describes two CAO designs that involve planning and implementing
a university event as part of the organizational purpose. The authors place
CAO within the broader literature of experiential learning, and delineate
two levels of analysis in experiential learning research – one that focuses
on the individual experience and the other on collective inquiry. Next, the
authors provide an overview of the "All Quadrants All Levels" (AQAL)
model from integral theory. They explain the distinction between lateral
development (i.e. increased skill at the current level of perception or
meaning-making) and vertical development (i.e. a qualitative shift in
our perception or meaning-making), and assert that the CAO approach
is useful for stimulating a student's vertical development. Finally, the
authors draw on their experience of facilitating CAO courses to illustrate
how the AQAL model is useful both for faculty, in making sense of CAO
designs, and for students, as an analytical tool. Specifically, they describe
two CAO designs that task students with planning, leading, organizing,
and controlling a sports event. Students in a sports event management
class work on an existing university event (e.g., Soccerfest), while students in a sports leadership class are tasked with developing their own
semester-long project.

**35. Bright, D. S., Turesky, E. F., Putzel, R., and Stang, T.
(2012). Professor as facilitator: Shaping an emerging, living
system of shared leadership in the classroom.** *Journal of
Leadership Education,* **11(1), 157–176.**

The authors explain how to facilitate and shape a class that is a complex,
adaptive and living system, and how to learn more about design principles to establish and sustain a shared leadership environment. The
authors help professors create a CAO with emergence, connectedness,
and feedback loops, and facilitate the students' learning experience as it
emerges. Through qualitative analysis of multiple CAO classes as well as
weekly memos written by students about their experience in the class, the

authors present three stages of emergence: early, middle, and late. They consider two aspects of each stage: the emergent developments that can be observed, and the actions that facilitators need to take to support the emergence in each stage. The early phase is marked by new structures, students' anxiety, and their underdeveloped forms of feedback, while the instructor facilitation focuses on building and explaining structures, nurturing a supportive environment, and building students' confidence with feedback. In the middle phase students are formalizing their structure, deepening their capacity for feedback, and becoming aware of their unique impact on the whole organization, while the facilitator is reinforcing the structure and facilitating authenticity. In the late stage students are reaching a convergence in task, process, and relationship as well as engaging in high-quality experiences. The facilitator focuses on encouraging reflection and facilitating an end to the course. Teaching CAO requires a different set of competencies than teaching in a traditional classroom. This article guides the facilitator through each stage of emergence and explains what facilitation techniques are needed to move between the stages.

36. **Conklin, T. A. (2013). Making it personal: The importance of student experience in creating autonomy-supportive classrooms for millennial learners. *Journal of Management Education*, 37(4), 499–538.**

Conklin outlines how CAO fits within the larger umbrella of student-centered learning. He provides a compelling argument that management educators must embrace learning methodologies that integrate thinking with action or "choose to relegate ourselves to the equivalent of the rotary dial phone" (p. 503). He reviews the literature on experience-based learning and drills down into three specific androgogies that hold promise for supporting greater student autonomy in the classroom: student-centered learning, problem-based learning, and CAO. The section on CAO includes a thoughtful discussion of the appropriate role of theory in the undergraduate classroom. Conklin underscores the benefits of CAO, including the emphasis on teams and networking, that have practical application in the world of work. He explains that autonomy-supportive classrooms, those in which the teacher has an orientation toward empowering rather than controlling students, result in greater motivation and self-esteem in the learner. The article concludes with a discussion of the characteristics of millennial students and an argument for why autonomy-supported classrooms are important for this group. This article provides a useful frame for "why" one would use CAO and "how" it fits within the experience-based learning domain.

37. **Bright, D. S., Caza, A., Turesky, E. F., Putzel, R., Nelson, E., and Luechtefeld, R. (2016). Constructivist meta-practices: When students design activities, lead others, and assess peers.** *Journal of Leadership Education*, **15(4), 75–99.**

The authors propose the term "meta-practice" to describe "a pedagogical element that is used across various teaching strategies" (p. 76). They identify three specific meta-practices relevant to a constructivist approach and illustrate how these are integrated within three common teaching strategies: problem-based learning, team-based learning, and CAO. The authors report the results of a study exploring the relationship between these three meta-practices and five outcomes for students: content knowledge, self-efficacy, self-awareness, engagement, and sense of community. All three meta-practices were significantly related to class engagement. The meta-practices of leading others and assessing peers were significant in predicting the remaining outcome variables of self-efficacy, self-awareness, and sense of community. Their results suggest that only one meta-practice, students designing learning activities, was a significant predictor of content knowledge. All three meta-practices were significantly related to class engagement. Implications for both practice and research are discussed. This is a unique article in that it is one of the few studies with empirical data related to the processes and outcomes related to CAO.

38. **Hendry, J. R., Hiller, T. B., Martin, E. C., and Boyd, N. M. (2017). Context and pedagogy: A quarter-century of change in an introductory management course.** *Journal of Management Education*, **41(3), 346–384.**

This article is an update on the evolution of the Management 101 CAO course (Miller, 1991), which has run from 1979 to the present. The authors, four professors currently teaching the course, clearly describe how the course is presently run and provide a detailed set of appendices showing its main elements: key stakeholders, the master schedule, chronology of a semester, evaluating student performance, and student perspectives. The appendices also include the practical pieces needed to implement the course. Hendry et al. provide an overview of changes that have taken place in the course as well as elements that have remained constant, including the underlying themes, pedagogies, and philosophies.

39.   Miller, J. A. (2017). Lessons from Management 101: Learning to manage ourselves. *Journal of Management Education,* **41(3), 335–345.**

Miller reflects on the process of teaching his signature CAO (Miller, 1991) that was started in 1979 and is still going strong today at Bucknell University in Pennsylvania. In this article Miller ponders the lessons they have learned by reflecting on three questions: Who needs to learn? What are the best practices for learning? and What are the essential elements that need to be learned? The "who" are undergraduate students with little, if any, business experience. The course is designed to inform and educate non-business (as well as business) majors on the basics of business and management. In response to the second question, best learning practice is a combination of lectures with the project/lab where students design and run their own complex business. Students learn by doing, and prove their understanding of concepts by putting them to work in a business. The third question (What do students need to learn?) relates to when students start designing and running their business and discover what they don't know. The professors of these courses have culled and shaped readings, teachings, and practical operational strategies and tools. They found that no textbook could guide them through the content piece of this class, that they had to know their topic areas broadly and deeply and draw from a number of resources (including each other) to bring together the content to support the learning experience in this course. The article elucidates the underlying values and goals of the course as well as years of an itera- tive learning process to make the course successful.

40.   London, M. B., and Van Buskirk, B. (2018). The co-created classroom: From teacher/student to mentor/apprentice. In J. Neal (ed.), *Handbook of Personal and Organizational Transformation* **(pp. 1051–1080). New York: Springer.**

The authors have designed a CAO that makes the coaching relationship between professor and students more formal. Their book chapter is a reflexive exploration of insights gained by London in his quest to create more meaningful relationships in the classroom. For instance, a discussion on the tension between authentically engaging in class activities while also maintaining enough distance is illuminated through a powerful example and reflexive insight for future practice. Another key insight is the realization that there are unspoken dynamics in the classroom – a complex mix of external influences that concern students – that must be named and embraced rather than ignored or treated as a distraction from the course content. The authors illustrate how the mentor/apprentice model was operationalized in a small undergraduate OB course by describing the micro-process of coaching a two-person student team as they developed a 75-minute session on culture. This forms the basis for exploring the classroom as a community of practice and treating students as teaching assistants rather than passive learners. The authors share four design interventions and discuss how each facilitated the shift to a co-created classroom: a poetry gallery; coaching for high-impact class sessions; creating virtuous cycles around student-facilitated sessions; and continuous evaluation of self, others, and the class. The significant contribution of this article is the explication of a role for the professor as an active coach and collaborator, a mid-point between being the sole teacher and abdicating teaching to students.

Appendix 1: OB Inc. Syllabus

[School Logo Here]
Organizational Behavior – OB Inc.
Semester, Year

Educator name:
Educator title:
Office location:
Office hours:
Organization (i.e. class) meeting times:
Group meetings: You will need to find time to meet weekly with your group.

Email:

Course catalog description
Three hours contact time per week. This course examines the complex and dynamic interactions of people and organizations in society. Particular focus will be on organizational theory, human perception, motivation, group dynamics, power, conflict, culture, leadership, organizational development, and managing change. *Prerequisite: i.e. Principles of Management.*

Required text
Neck, C. P., Houghton, J. D., and Murray, E. L. (2018). *Organizational behavior: A skill-building approach.* SAGE Publications.

WELCOME TO OB INC.!

Course Objectives

This course is designed to present the basic ideas, concepts, and theories of organizational behavior in a systematic and integrative fashion so that by the end of the course you should understand the complexities of managing people in modern organizations. Through gaining this understanding, you will also develop skills necessary to manage people effectively.

The course objectives are for students to:

1. Identify and define key concepts and theories related to organizational behavior and leadership.
2. Apply key concepts and theories to examples from OB Inc. to analyze their experiences.
3. Critique and discriminate between applications of key concepts and theories.
4. Design structures and learning activities related to key concepts and theories.

In the process of meeting these cognitive domain learning objectives, the following affective domain learning objectives will also be met. Students will:

5. Receive and provide feedback.
6. Initiate action in ambiguous contexts.
7. Demonstrate responsibility for outcomes that impact the organization.
8. Differentiate between priorities to meet the needs of the organization.
9. Compare intended outcomes with actual performance.
10. Synthesize relational values with operational efficiency in addressing conflict.
11. Practice exercising influence.
12. Practice self-awareness and self-regulation.

Please note: Reading this syllabus leaves some students feeling a bit overwhelmed. DON'T WORRY! Most students have a *fantastic experience* as they successfully complete this course. You will be amazed at what we accomplish together. We will build the organization of our class step-by-step as we learn about management and organizational behavior. Just stick with it and all will fall into place and start to make sense.

Our Organizational Learning Task

Our task is to help you discover the basic components, processes, and wholeness of organizing. OB Inc. is the name of the organization that we will build and run together. We will generate learning through service that builds a living organization in which our capacity to work together continually grows.

My approach to this course draws on several traditions of teaching that reach back over 50 years and have been refined through long trial and error. It combines the best of leading teaching techniques and will be unusual for many of you. This class also puts into practice the lessons learned by students before you. Together, we will generate lessons that will reshape future generations of this class. You have a responsibility not only to each other but also to future leaders and managers who will stand on your shoulders.

The following **principles** will guide our efforts:

- Powerful organizing dynamics emerge when people become as concerned for others as they are for themselves – hence we will emphasize service-based learning.
- Leading in the learning organization requires constant proactive effort.
- Understanding leadership, management, and organizational behavior comes from experience: we learn by managing, leading, and/or changing organizational behavior.
- Effective organizations draw on the strengths of everyone.
- Mastery of a topic comes from both learning and teaching it.
- Responsible self-teaching and learning are the lifeblood of a leader and manager.

Our Organizational Structure

The vehicle for teaching this class is the creation of a true learning organization where every member has an opportunity to be empowered. Every effective organization is comprised of a number of tasks. You will succeed by practicing the skills in each of these learning modes, and you will learn by taking responsibility for the creation and functioning of this class. The most important rule is to **be creative**, **have fun**, and **learn** along the way.

Senior manager

As the professor, I am the OB Inc. senior manager. My task is to lead you in learning. I have ultimate responsibility for everything that takes place in this course. I am delegating many of the details for carrying out this responsibility to you. I have a penchant for helping you succeed. Much of my work will take place behind the scenes. I will learn as much, or more, from you as you will from me.

If you need to contact me, my first choice is email. Please schedule an appointment if you need to see me in person, even during office hours.

Please note that I view it as my job to **facilitate your learning** – NOT to lecture at you. OB Inc. is NOT an organization modeled on a business corporation, but rather an organization that is designed to effectively and powerfully cultivate the knowledge to be developed from this class. Some of you will view this class as a radical departure from the normal model of university education. I know from experience that, compared to simple lectures and tests, this is a superior forum for learning.

Learning teams

The basic unit of OB Inc. is a learning team of up to five individuals from diverse perspectives and backgrounds. Most of your work takes place within this team, and your team will need to meet outside of organizational meetings (i.e. class), especially to plan for your teaching responsibilities.

Students as managers and leaders

To succeed in this class you must learn to function as both a **manager** and **leader**. First, there are several management responsibilities that must be carried out if our organization is to function properly: taking attendance, gathering records, arranging tables and chairs, etc. In addition, we need to ensure that every OB Inc. member has an adequate opportunity to learn theories of management and organizational behavior. In a normal classroom the professor assumes most of these tasks. However, in OB Inc. we will divide these tasks and functions.

In addition, each of you should act as a **self-motivated** leader. You are exercising leadership when you push yourself to function at the edge of your comfort zone. You will need to identify your strengths, areas that you wish to develop in yourself, and **compile a service record** of activities that demonstrate your leadership contributions to this organization. As you demonstrate what you are learning through your leadership in this organization, you will develop important skills that will stick with you for a long time.

Class procedure

This class teaches about organizations by functioning as a real, living organization. This is not a simulation. You must be able to understand how the knowledge affects you as a functioning individual within a living system.

The semester is divided into four sections. In the first section I will guide the organization, but in subsequent sections students will carry the responsibility for managing the function of the organization. While working under the supervision of the senior manager (your professor), each person will have an opportunity to lead activities within the team, and each team will have two opportunities to present a chapter to the entire organization. Soon, you will own this organization and its function. (I have had instances where the organization's meetings carried on without me.)

The text and course are intended to be highly interactive. We create activities that invoke multiple learning styles. There should be something for everyone in the class meetings. The standard chapter presentation includes your team creating and taking the members of the organization through an experiential activity to explore the topic, and then leading an in-depth debrief through which members integrate and deepen their learning of the topic.

Typically, each organization meeting will consist of administrative items such as grading, observations, announcements, and service activities; a chapter presentation with an experiential activity and debrief; and organization-wide discussions and decision-making time. I encourage you to be proactive and to find innovative ways to fulfill your responsibilities. Again, the rule is to be creative, have fun, and learn along the way.

Making mistakes in the process of running our organization is OK! In fact, I expect you to make mistakes because mistakes present an opportunity for learning. We appreciate the wholeness of organizing – good and bad. Repeating the same mistake, however, is a problem; you are expected to learn from your mistakes, and make different mistakes next time.

Grading

Every member in an organization, in everything they do, affects others. The grading system is designed to give you insight into *others' points of views* and *greater self-awareness* about *how your actions influence others*. I suggest that you **worry less about your grade and more about your learning**. In addition, the point distribution below may be subject to change, based on the decisions made in our organizational meetings.

Table A1.1   *Assessment structure for OB Inc.*

Assignment	%	
Quizzes individual	15	Individual
Quizzes group	10	Team
Chapter presentations *(recommended by Feedback Team)*	10	Team
Service (5%) and participation/attendance (10%) *(recommended by Service Excellence Team)*	15	Individual
Team member feedback *(recommended by Feedback Team)*	5	Individual
Journaling grade *(recommended by Journaling Team)*	10	Individual
Group development grade *(recommended by Group Development Team)*	5	Team
Team performance grade *(recommended by Team Performance Team)*	5	Team
Personal application essays (2)	15	Individual
Final presentation	10	Team
TOTAL	100	

60% of your grade is individual, 40% comes from teamwork.

60% of your grade is recommended by peers, 40% by the senior manager.

Personal preparation, reading, and quizzes

In most courses learning ends with taking a test. In this course the learning begins by demonstrating you understand the basic terms and ideas by taking a quiz. The intention is that you come to meetings prepared, which will translate into energy-filled and fun sessions.

At the beginning of every week there is a specified time for reading quizzes. So, each week you need to come to our meetings prepared to take a reading quiz of between five and 12 questions. Each of these quizzes will first be taken individually and then afterward will be taken together with your team.

Each reading quiz will include an appeal process which is described at the end of this syllabus, and will be reviewed after the first quiz.

Chapter presentations (experiential learning activities)

Your team will have an opportunity to create learning activities for others in the organization. You will help us master and/or apply concepts from the book. The textbook contains a number of learning activities that you need to review as a team and decide if you are going to use. You may decide to make up your own activity(ies). If you do, it needs to adhere to the content of the chapter while helping the members of the organization to actively engage in the content. **You must meet with the Senior Manager to discuss the activity before you present, and allow enough time to revise your plans if necessary.** You will share accountability for the work of preparing and presenting. You need to think creatively about what can be done. You can share media clips. You might search for games related to your chapter topic (i.e. "games for organizational structure") to see what you can find. The *Journal of Management Education* (https://journals.sagepub.com/home/jme) has lots of articles on experiential activities for almost any topic in our course. You can ask me for more resources and ideas for teaching as well. You will be evaluated on your presentations by a rubric that you as an organization will approve.

Service

Each of you is expected to contribute through service to build a culture of learning in our class. Service is an expression of your willingness to exercise leadership, contribute to a team, develop high-quality relationships, share your insights, and give feedback. These activities also contribute significantly to your learning because they provide you with opportunities to put theory into practice.

To complete this requirement, each of you should exercise **initiative**, and demonstrate **courage**, **engagement**, or **thoughtful** effort to find ways to help each other and the senior manager. Compile a record of your activities that demonstrates how you are working to be highly engaged, to push yourself as a leader, and to make a contribution to a culture of learning in this organization. In your service record, write down **any** activity you do in our meetings, or for the organization outside of our meetings, that requires "initiative, courage, engagement, or thoughtful effort." The grade for service depends on **time**, **variety**, and **effort**.

You should keep track of your service on a service activity record (posted in the LMS). The form requires that you describe your activity and get a signature from a classmate certifying that your action had impact on others. If you simply show up to our meetings and make small, consistent contributions, your record is easily developed. More weight can be given to activities that require more effort.

The Service Team will collect your service records at the end of each reporting period and give you a recommended grade. **No more than half of your entries may come from any one activity**.

Your service grade is determined as follows: 30 or more light activities = excellent; 20-29 =good; 11-19 = satisfactory; 10 or fewer = inadequate.

The activities listed below are examples:

- Give an impromptu presentation, lead an impromptu discussion, or lead a decision-making process.
- Demonstrate leadership by organizing an activity on your own initiative.
- Provide observations about the organization in the last few minutes of a meeting period (sign up for this with the Culture and Coordination Team).
- Create a chapter study document for your teammates to help them study for the quiz.
- Help others with their service projects.
- Demonstrate exemplary leadership.
- Review extra drafts of the personal application essays for members of your team or other teams.
- Go the extra mile to provide classmates with exemplary feedback (above and beyond what is assigned).
- Coordinate any activity for your team's area of responsibility.
- Post additional, meaningful responses to others' journal entries.
- Do **anything else** that will help the class function at a higher level.

These activities that can be accomplished with other students:

- Develop name recognition and getting to know one another's activities
- Room setup
- Celebration times
- Organize a study session (not just attend one)
- Propose any other project that will contribute to the learning environment of the organization.

Participation/attendance

Absences are unexcused except for official absences for school activities or severe illness for which you have a letter from your doctor. Being more than five minutes late to an organization meeting constitutes an absence. Since we only meet once a week, each meeting is actually worth a week of the semester. You have one free unexcused absence for the semester. After that, each absence will deduct 4 percent from your final grade until you reach the maximum of 10 percent allocated for attendance. Missing four weeks will result in failing the course. Your participation grade will be suggested to the senior manager by the Service Team based on these guidelines.

Team Performance

Each team will have a set of tasks that must be completed and will be evaluated on how well these are executed. The Performance Team will ensure your team receives this assessment and feedback.

Journaling

The organization journal will be important for the final assignment of the course, which requires you to analyze aspects of our organization's history. At least once each week, the Journaling Team will give you an opportunity to write about your experiences in the organization. Questions to address in your journal entries will be posted in the public discussion thread either during or immediately after class. Your entries should not be less than 150 words, and you will be expected to respond to others' posts. The Journaling Team may also ask you to participate in assessing others' journal entries.

Personal application essays

You will write two (2) individual personal application essays. You will discuss your own personal growth as a leader, follower, and functional contributing organizational member. You will use three major concepts from the text, explain the concepts using one scholarly resource for each (you need three sources), and apply them to specific observations of your behavior, experience, and personal growth in the organization. The paper should be 3–4 pages long, double-spaced APA style with a cover page (no abstract). The structure is:

1. Introduction
2. Concept #1

    a.   Definition

    b.   Resource – description of resource and connection to your concept

    c.   Application

3. Concept #2

    a.   Definition

    b.   Resource – description of resource and connection to your concept

    c.   Application

4. Concept #3

    a.   Definition

    b.   Resource – description of resource and connection to your concept

    c.   Application

5. Conclusion

6. References

The process is outlined below:

- **Write a draft** and **post it** in the LMS by the deadline designated in the course schedule.
- Read your teammates' essays and **give them feedback** on their essay by the deadline designated in the course schedule.
- **Revise** your essay, drawing on the feedback you have received from teammates.
- Submit the **final draft** in the LMS by the deadline.

Final presentation: Overview of the course

The final exam in this course is a presentation that will require you to work with your team to demonstrate both mastery of course concepts and your ability as a presenter. As a team, you will perform an analysis of the history of this class as an organization, using concepts that we have studied. The intention is to present your analysis as a holistic story using multiple presenters. Each member of the team should select one topic related to this analysis and prepare a 3–4-minute presentation. In total your team will have 15–20 minutes to present on exam day, with each person presenting on one topic, analyzing one aspect of the history of the organization for 3–4 minutes.

Table A1.2   *Schedule and action checklist for OB Inc. – Semester, year*

Week # (Dates)	Reading	Assignments
Establishing the Foundation of our Organization – Professor Leads		
1–3 (Dates)	Week 1 (before class): • Class Syllabus • Ch. 2 – Diversity and Individual Differences Week 2 (before class): • Ch. 1 – Why Organizational Behavior Matters • Team Description and Tasks Week 3 (before class): • Ch 3 – Perception and Learning	Week #1 (before class) • Complete personality test BEFORE the first class https://www.16personalities.com/free-personality-test Week #2 (before class) • Meet with your team to complete group work (provided on the LMS) • Prepare for individual and group quiz on the syllabus, Ch. 1 and 2 Week #3 (before class): • Meet with your team to complete group work (provided on the LMS) • Prepare for quiz on Ch. 3
Individual Processes – Students Take Responsibility for the Organization		
4–6 (Dates)	• Ch. 4 Emotions, Attitudes and Stress • Ch. 5 Motivation: Concepts and Theoretical Perspectives • Ch. 6 Motivation: Practices and Applications	• Prepare your chapter presentation • Prepare for individual and group quiz every week • Write journal entries for each chapter • Complete service and update record • Meet with teams to complete group work
Teams and Teamwork – Students in Charge		
7–11 (Dates)	• Ch. 7 Teams • Ch. 8 Decision Making, Creativity, and Innovation • Ch. 9 Ethics and Social Responsibility in Organizations • Ch. 10 Effective Communication • Ch. 11 Trust, Conflict, and Negotiation	• Personal application essay draft due _____ (week 7) • Personal application essay final due _____ (week 8) • Each team completes the midterm team improvement assignment (change initiative); due _____ (week 9) • Prepare your chapter presentation • Prepare for individual and group quiz every week • Write journal entries for each chapter • Complete service and update record • Meet with teams to complete group work

Week # (Dates)	Reading	Assignments
Students in Charge – Leadership and Organizations		
12–15 (Dates – this includes spring break or Thanksgiving; plan on two chapters one week)	• Ch. 12 Leadership Perspectives • Ch. 13 Influence, Power, and Politics • Ch. 14 Organizations and Culture • Ch. 15 Organizational Change and Structure	• Prepare your chapter presentation • Prepare for individual and group quiz every week • Write journal entries for each chapter • Complete service and update record • Meet with teams to complete group work • Personal application essay draft due _____(week 14) • Personal application essay final due Friday midnight week 15
16 (Dates)	Final oral presentations – celebration!	Final presentations will take place during exam week in place of a final exam.

Readiness Assessment Test:

Guidelines for preparing successful appeals:

Appeals are granted when they demonstrate that you understood the concept(s) but there was ambiguity in the question or ambiguity in the reading material that caused you to miss the question.

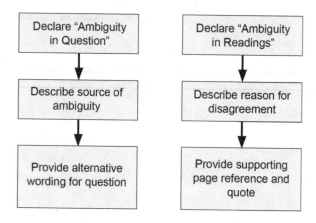

Impact of appeals on test scores:

When an appeal is accepted on a question that a group has missed (no individual appeals will be accepted):

1. It "counts" i.e., the points missed will be added to:

- their group score.
- the score of any individual in the group who answered the same as the group
- only those groups that appeal.

2. Group member(s) who had the original correct answer will continue to receive credit on the question.

Appendix 2: Service record

Activities that required initiative, courage, engagement, or thoughtful effort to help us build a culture of learning.

Team Name:_____

Name:_____

	Date	Service description	Influence on others	Student signature (observed the influence of this behavior)
1				
2				
3				
4				
5				
6				
7				
8				
9				
10				
11				
12				
13				
14				
15				
16				
17				
18				
19				
20				
21				
22				

	Date	Service description	Influence on others	Student signature (observed the influence of this behavior)
23				
24				
25				
26				
27				
28				
29				
30				

Appendix 3: Feedback to team members

Instructions

- Prepare a written statement for every member of your team by answering the questions below.
- Follow the instructions given by the Feedback Team to turn a copy of your feedback in for evaluation. You will need to keep a copy for yourself.
- During your team time, or during organization meetings, if time is allotted, share your feedback with each teammate verbally and give them a copy of your written feedback.
- Be sure to include the following on your submission:

Your name: _____

Date of report: _____

Team name: _____

Team member you are evaluating: _____

Questions to Address in your Individual Team Member Feedback

- **Contribution to your learning.** Share with your teammate specific information about what he/she does to contribute to your learning in this class. How does each teammate use their strengths in class? How does each teammate influence your thinking?

For example: Billy, since we have opposite learning styles, you contribute to my learning by talking about how you understand the material the senior manager talks about. You specifically helped me see the difference between collaboration and cooperation.

- **Contribution to the team.** Share with your teammate your perspective about the positive contributions he/she makes to the team. Does it make a difference in your team dynamic when they miss a meeting of the organization? Do they enact a norm, or do something, that makes your team function better?

  For example: Betty, our team is grateful that you always step up to be our unappointed scribe. I love that you take that burden off us and we know that you will keep track of all our ideas and be able to read them back to us when it's time to create our final answers.

- **Suggestions.** In what ways can your teammate improve or build on those things that they do well? Or how can they change some aspect of performance that is missing? How can this improvement be made? Describe in very specific language.

  For example: Veronica, continue to practice active listening. Try to use a different technique each day to see if you can change our team dynamic just by how you respond to us. Continue to offer your unique suggestions that help us think outside the normal box. Get even more creative and help us do the same.

An Example of Outstanding Feedback

Morgan, you contribute to my learning by showing the courage to speak up in our group. You have said several times that it is hard for you to speak up because we are so noisy. When you do though, you always have something valuable to add. One instance was when we worked on our "Chapter Presentation". You saw several examples of confrontation (conflict style) that no one else did. We have learned how to "make space" for you. This gives me practice for the real world as well because I will work with other people similar to you. You contribute to our team by using your active listening skills in every class. We all know that when we come to class and need to vent before the lesson starts, you will be the one to talk to. You never seem overwhelmed by how loud we can be and you give us the space we need to change our attitudes. Specifically, two weeks ago when it was raining, you came to class happy anyway and let us whine about the rain, but your positive mood was contagious and we soon forgot about the rain outside because we were having such a good time. One suggestion would be for you to create a non-verbal signal to tell us you would like to talk. Since it can be hard for us to listen, your voice often gets lost in the noise of us talking. Maybe hold up your hand to ask us to slow down or write your ideas down and pass them around the table. You have valuable contributions for our team and you need to make us listen to you in a way that works. We will also work on "making space" for you more often now that we have learned about that concept.

Assessment Rubric for Feedback to Teammates

The Feedback Team will use the following rubric to assess the feedback you provide to your teammates.

Grading Criteria:	Rating				
Did the student generate feedback for each member of his/her team?	NO		YES		
The feedback was written in complete sentences and was of sufficient length to be meaningful.	1	2	3	4	5
The statements include specific positive examples about contributions to the team – what the teammates do well.	1	2	3	4	5
The statements include specific language about how the teammates might improve or have even more influence.	1	2	3	4	5
The feedback connected to the topics we have learned or real-world implications of the behaviors discussed.	1	2	3	4	5
1 = inadequate, 2 = poor, 3 = average, 4 = good, 5 = outstanding					

Appendix 4: Team development evaluation

As a team read the statements below, discuss, and circle the number that most accurately describes your team at this time. Keep in mind that your team is starting in the forming stage, and you should have a number of these items that you score low on at the beginning of the semester because you are still working on them. As your team develops during the semester, you will improve on some of these items. To show improvement throughout the semester on your team development, you will need to record areas of improvement (low scores) early in the semester. Your grade will be based on improvement throughout the semester, not on having a perfect score. A perfect score at the beginning of the semester shows disingenuous answers since no team will score high on all these measures in the forming stage of team development.

You may use this rubric to measure team development or you may use the assessment tool found in the Lencioni text (2012, p. 114).

Team name:_____
Date:_____

Use the following key to respond to each statement:

- 1 = Disagree strongly
- 2 = Disagree to some extent
- 3 = Agree to some extent
- 4 = Agree strongly

1.	Members are clear about their team descriptions, tasks, and role in the organization.	1	2	3	4
2.	Individual members are given specific assignments that match their abilities.	1	2	3	4
3.	The group has an open communication structure that allows all the members to participate.	1	2	3	4
4.	Team meetings involve the whole team and are productive.	1	2	3	4

5.	Members give each other constructive feedback.	1	2	3	4
6.	The group uses feedback about its effectiveness to make improvements.	1	2	3	4
7.	The group spends time defining and discussing problems it must solve.	1	2	3	4
8.	The group uses effective decision-making strategies.	1	2	3	4
9.	The group accepts members who behave differently as long as their behavior is perceived as helpful to task accomplishment.	1	2	3	4
10.	Group norms encourage high performance, quality, and success.	1	2	3	4
11.	Group norms encourage members to admit mistakes and share their weaknesses.	1	2	3	4
12.	The group is highly cohesive and cooperative.	1	2	3	4
13.	Periods of conflicts are frequent but brief.	1	2	3	4
14.	The group uses effective conflict management strategies.	1	2	3	4
15.	Group tasks require members to work together.	1	2	3	4

Include a collective response to the following questions in your submission to the Team Development Team:

1. Indicate your total score out of 60:_____

2. Using Tuckman and Jensen's (1977) five stages of development, describe your stage of development, using examples from your team interactions to support your opinion.

References

Lencioni, P. M. (2012), *The Five Dysfunctions of a Team: Team Assessment*, San Francisco, CA: Wiley & Sons.

Tuckman, B. W. and M. A. C. Jensen (1977), 'Stages of small-group development revisited', *Group and Organization Studies*, **2** (4), 419–427.

Appendix 5: Team performance evaluation

The Performance Team will use the rubric provided (you are free to change the rubric as you see fit) to oversee the process of evaluating the performance of each team. You need to lead the process of each team evaluating all other teams in the organization on a regular basis. You also need to ensure that each team has appropriate goals and that they are meeting these goals.

Performance evaluations account for five percent of your overall grade in this course. The average of the scores your team receives from the five other teams in the organization will determine your grade for this performance evaluation. Every member of a group will receive the same performance score. There will be three performance evaluations in total throughout the semester, meaning that each individual performance score you receive accounts for 1.67 percent of your grade in this course.

Team Performance Evaluation Rubric

	10–9	8–7	6–5	4–0
Contribution	**Excellent:** Group excels in fulfilling its role by contributing superior quality work to the organization.	**Average:** Group meets expectations for fulfilling its role by contributing quality work to the organization.	**Below Average:** Group is inconsistent in fulfilling expectations for its role and/or is not consistent in contributing quality work to the organization.	**Needs Significant Improvement:** Group is detracting from the organization in this capacity.
Cooperation	**Excellent:** Group promotes organizational cohesion through superior communication and effective coordination between groups in accordance with its group role.	**Average:** Group contributes to organizational cohesion through clear communication and coordination between groups in accordance with its group role.	**Below Average:** Group is inconsistent in communicating and coordinating between groups in accordance with its group role.	**Needs Significant Improvement:** Group detracts from the organization in this capacity.
Leadership	**Excellent:** Group demonstrates superior initiative and is able to effectively direct/guide the organization through activities and tasks that pertain to its role.	**Average:** Group demonstrates initiative and is able to direct/guide the organization through activities and tasks that pertain to its role.	**Below Average:** Group demonstrates inconsistent initiative to direct/guide the organization through activities and tasks that pertain to its role.	**Needs Significant Improvement:** Group detracts from the organization in this capacity.
Goals	**Excellent:** Group is making excellent progress toward meeting its goals.	**Average:** Group is making consistent progress toward meeting its goals.	**Below Average:** Group is making below average progress towards meeting its goals.	**Needs Significant Improvement:** Group is not taking steps in meeting its goals.

Appendix 6: Detailed instructions for week one

The first 7.5–9 hours of the course constitute the first phase of the CAO class. This first phase is educator intensive; you will be in charge of the class for this first phase, and will turn responsibility over to the students for the next two phases. The purpose of the first phase of your CAO is to establish the ground rules of the organization as well as help students prepare for this course format and their upcoming responsibilities.

WEEK ONE (FIRST 2.5–3 HOURS)

Before Class

- Assign students to complete the free online version of the Type Indicator (MBTI) personality test (or another assessment that you will use to help students self-reflect as well as get to know one another on a deeper basis, such as Kolb's Learning Style Inventory). Students need to come to class with their four MBTI letters.
- Assign them to read Chapter 2 of Neck et al. (2018) before class.
- Arrange seats in a circle before students arrive. This format heightens awareness that something is fundamentally different in this course. Ultimately, students will decide how to configure the room to suit their needs. Meeting in a circle during these first weeks demonstrates that we will make the space work for us, and not vice versa.

Icebreaker Activity

Lead one or two icebreaker activities at the beginning of class to set the tone of an active environment and the importance of relationships in this course. Focus these activities on getting to know names especially. Ask for volunteers to lead these *getting-to-know-you* activities in the next two weeks of the course. It is important that students know each other by name since they will work closely together throughout the semester.

First Class Discussion

We advise starting the first class period by sitting in a circle. This establishes from the beginning that we are not in a traditional class and don't plan to run this in a traditional way. The discussion prompt can be "Tell us who you are, why you are here, and what you hope to gain from this class," which gets the discussion started. Rather than working your way around the circle, have a volunteer go first, and when they are finished they point to someone else in the circle (naming them if they know their name) to go next. This keeps it interesting and helps students stay focused. Depending on how large or small the class is, you may choose to ask a second question.

Conclude this activity by asking them what they observed during the activity. They will usually focus on surface and obvious observations like "There are three football players in the class" or they may focus on the themes of why people are here. The goal of this activity, in addition to furthering relationship building, is to introduce the norm of surfacing the thinking and feeling that underpin observable phenomena. As you keep asking "What else did you observe?" you are probing for observations about everyone's experience in the circle. Someone might offer that they felt nervous, or that they interpreted the behaviors of others as being nervous or excited. You can test that out by asking "How many of you are nervous?" or "Who is excited to be here?" Push this conversation further until they can talk not only about the task at hand but also the feelings and experiences they are having. During this activity, they are learning from what YOU DO, from the presence that you bring into the classroom: your emotional state, the assumptions you have, the openness to their experience, and the care you demonstrate for them as human beings. These are all part of the model for how they will learn to operate in this class and in an organization.

Students' emotions (fear, anxiety, excitement, etc.) are all sources of feedback that can flow into the organization as data. In this exercise, and throughout OB Inc., each person is trying to make sense of this new experience and is reacting in a different way. We encourage students to become aware of these through the conversations that happen in the first weeks. We are essentially surfacing what is not normally noticed in a classroom – the emotional climate, the emotional contagion, etc. In these first weeks, your goal is to model the kinds of attitudes and actions that you want students to emulate as they begin to lead the class.

Brief introduction to the course

Explain briefly the history and purpose of organizational behavior, and why it's an important topic for management students. Also, explain briefly the methodology of teaching the course (CAO), and why you are choosing to teach it this way.

You might use a simple metaphor to articulate to students the value of CAO: one does not learn how to play basketball by memorizing the rules and dissecting how others play; you need to play the game. Similarly, learning the nuances of management and organizational behavior requires stepping into the reality of organizational life. CAO enables a holistic, integrative, and developmental experience.

MBTI Activity

This activity lays the foundation for a conversation about diversity, and ultimately for choosing diverse teams. The first element of this activity involves students meeting with others who are similar to them to discuss their similarities. This is followed by an exploration of the differences between their group and other groups. The whole process contributes to moving the class through the forming stage of group development and establishes the foundation for working with and through others.

Make sure that everyone has their four letters for their personality test. Do a brief review of the Myers-Briggs four elements and the four main types: SJ (Sensing-Judging), SP (Sensing-Perceiving), NT (Intuitive-Thinking), NF (Intuitive-Feeling).

Break students into groups based on which two letters they have in their personality: SJ, SP, NT, NF. This will put people who have similar personalities together. Give each group a flip chart and pen, and ask them to write their answers to the following questions on the chart (15 min): 1) What do you wish others understood better about you and people like you? 2) How can someone be a better teammate by adapting to your type? Students only share two out of the four letters, so they are trying to discover what they have in common with one another in this activity, and they are working on how to express that to the other groups.

Each group gets the chance to: 1) share their answers to the questions; and 2) field questions from other groups about their personality (30 min). Once the group shares their answers encourage other students to think about if this person were on their team, what questions would they have? For example, a task-oriented student (SJ) might ask a relationship-oriented (IF) student "How would you like to be managed, what motivates you, do you like praise in public or private?", etc. The purpose is to get students to think about how they might need to apply their own communication and work patterns to fit those of teammates who are different from them.

Ask students if they think it's a good idea to put people with similar personalities all on the same team. Through discussion let them come to the conclusion that it would be best to have mixed teams, and that each personality type brings a different strength to the team.

Create Diverse Teams

Lead Exercise 2.2 from the text (Neck et al., 2018, p. 61) to get students to recognize the difference between surface level and deep level diversity. This activity gets students thinking about diversity and why it is important on teams. Once that activity is completed, lead them in a discussion to identify the levels of diversity present in the class. This can be as simple as asking them to identify examples of surface-level and deeper-level diversity that they notice among class members. Writing these on the board will help them remember to address these points of diversity as they form their teams.

Referring to Chapter 2 of the text (Neck et al., 2018), briefly explain the science behind diverse teams and ask students to form the most diverse teams possible for this class. In preparation for this, place six sheets of paper on the walls of the classroom, as spread out as possible. Number each sheet from one to six. Ask students to gather in the middle of the class in their MBTI groups. Point out the six sheets of paper and explain these are intended as spaces for the groups they will form. Next, ask them how they will go about finding the first member of each team. Ask students to engage in a group process of creating the most diverse teams possible. As they begin to discuss and work through how to form teams you may need to remind them that, if they know anyone well or if they have worked with anyone in a team before, they should avoid being on the same team here (i.e. no football players together, no roommates or friends together, etc.). This is a bit of an awkward process as you haven't assigned anyone to lead. Allow the students to struggle through this one, encouraging them to keep asking questions.

Once the teams are formed, ask students to once again take a look at the teams and see if there are any swaps that need to be made to ensure that the teams are as diverse as possible. For example, students might notice that two best friends are on the same team and this needs to be changed.

Depending on how much class time is left, you can allow the teams some time to sit together and get to know each other a bit, or you can assign their team homework for the week and dismiss them. Placing the homework for the week on the LMS helps with clarity for the students as there is a lot happening in this first week. Remember to get volunteers to lead get to know you activities if you haven't already.

Team Meeting Assignment Week One

- Decide on a place to meet; you can meet anywhere on campus. Let me know where your team meeting place is so I can join you from time to time (link to Google sheet).
- Spend at least 10 minutes on each person in your group really getting to know them. Everyone asks questions.
  - 1st person - set your watch for 10 min and just learn more about that person. Then go around the group with 10 min for each person (if you have more than 3 people in your group you can do 5–7 minutes each).
  - You can use these questions as a guide: https://lifehacks.io/20 -questions-to-get-to-know-someone/.
- Remember the homework for this week:
  - Read the syllabus, Intro, Ch. 1 and Ch. 2.
  - Be ready for the quiz in week two on all of this material.

Here is some other group work for you this week:

- Read all team descriptions and think about which ones your team would like (URL or hyperlink to team descriptions).
  - Next week you will negotiate with other teams for the role you want, so be ready with a 1st, 2nd, and 3rd choice of which team role your team wants to take on.
- Think about which chapters you want to teach.
  - Check the schedule to see what chapters we will be covering (URL or hyperlink to action checklist).
  - We will be using this document for each team to choose one chapter to present in the first round and one chapter in the

syllabus, you will notice that 15 percent of the course grade is for individual chapter quizzes and 10 percent is for group chapter quizzes. We have students take the quiz individually first (either with paper and pencil or electronically through the learning management system/LMS), then the teams take the quiz together (again, via paper and pencil or electronically through the LMS). This is a form of team-based learning (TBL), specifically the Readiness Assurance Test (RAT). For more information on TBL visit http://www.teambasedlearning.org/. During the team quiz, students are able to check if their answers are correct. When they check their answer, if it is correct the first time they receive full points. For each time they check and are incorrect they lose one point. The conversation and debate around topics is an element of peer teaching and ensures that students come away with a deepened understanding of the main chapter concepts. In this first week, we formulate a quiz that covers the syllabus as well as Chapters 1 and 2 of the text.

Again, it is critical to frame for students the "why" behind the quizzes: (1) this form of learning only works if students come into class fully prepared; (2) the individual quiz tests whether you personally are prepared and have done the reading; (3) the group quiz gives you a chance to learn from and teach your peers as you take the quiz together and discuss the answers. Explain the mechanics of the quizzes: How does the individual quiz work? How does the group quiz work? How will they be graded, etc. See the appeal process as it is stated at the end of the syllabus and review it with the students.

Team Negotiation for Roles

Set up a Google sheet with each team number (1–6) vertically on the left and the team names horizontally across the top. Allow all students access to the document and show it on the screen. Have each team enter their 1st, 2nd, and 3rd preference for team responsibilities for the semester. When all teams have entered their preferences let them know that they need to negotiate with one another to come to an agreement. This is messy, and sometimes gets tense. The role of the educator is to keep asking questions. Students may have clarifying questions about the team descriptions and how they are implemented. When they ask, giving them an overview of the team responsibilities helps them understand what kinds of things they would be doing if they took on this team role. Refrain from giving too many details at this point as there is quite a bit of ambiguity in each team description. You may also want to remind students that there are options. For example, two teams who want the same role may agree to switch team roles at midterm.

Now that the teams have their assigned team description, allow them time in their teams (10 min) to discuss what they will need to do to fulfill it successfully. You can also have them prepare a short description of their team, and how they will contribute to the functioning of the organization. If you do this you can go around and have each team share out their synopsis, and allow other teams to ask them questions.

Team Negotiation for Chapters

Put up another Google sheet on the screen with chapter presentations and related dates for each vertically on the left, and team names horizontally across the top. First, have teams identify what chapters they have been assigned in their team description and fill out their assigned chapters on the spreadsheet. Next, have teams enter their 1st, 2nd, and 3rd choices, remembering that they will want to teach one chapter before midterms and one chapter after. Now introduce another negotiating session over the chapters. Allow the students to decide together who is teaching what. There is usually less tension over this negotiation since they don't usually feel too passionate about any particular chapters.

Discussion of Teaching Responsibilities

As it dawns on students that they will be teaching the content in the class, they will have both questions and preconceived ideas about what that will look like. Generally, students will think that they need to prepare a lecture on their chapter. Lecturing is not the purpose of the learning session, and preconditioned ideas of teaching need to be addressed here. You can do this in a number of ways. You may want to lead a discussion around the best learning experiences they have had, inside or outside of a classroom. On the whiteboard, make notes of the common elements. Facilitate a discussion around how the chapter presentations in this class could mirror their best learning experiences.

Help students understand what experiential learning is: to move beyond the knowledge acquisition they have done in preparation for the class session. Because of the assigned reading and the individual and group quizzes, they will know the basic concepts when they walk into class. The purpose of time in class together is to practice applying these concepts, deepen our understanding of how and when the concepts work, and when they don't. Therefore, explain to students that they need to carefully plan and lead experiential activities for the whole class. These activities need to closely relate to the concepts in their assigned chapters. Furthermore, the debrief time is of utmost importance to extract the most learning from the experiences. Spend some time helping students understand what constitutes an effective debrief, and explain that you plan to spend time with each team before their first presentation refining the activities as well as helping them to improve the debrief questions.

Class-wide Discussion on Class Expectations

Lead students through Exercise 3.1 on page 88 of the text (Neck et al., 2018) to facilitate a discussion around perceptions of the course so far. After this activity, have students get into their newly formed groups. Have them form questions they want to ask you about the course (the why, specifics, etc.). You may want to discuss the concept of a psychological contract (Neck et al., 2018, p. 306), explaining that we are building a new psychological contract that is different than that found in most courses. This is a time for you and the students to come to an agreement about the specifics of this course, and acknowledge that you will both be playing different roles than in a traditional classroom. Let the groups take turns asking you questions about the course until all of their questions are answered. This is also your chance to ask students the questions you want.

Tolerance of Ambiguity Exercise

Design an exercise around completing and discussing the tolerance of ambiguity (TOA) concept (Budner, 1962). The class mirrors the kind of ambiguity experienced in a new job or work environment; the presence of ambiguity is an important part of CAO. Discussing class members' willingness and ability to deal with ambiguity will help them expect, prepare, and strive for higher tolerance levels; given advance notice, students are more equipped to embrace the ambiguity inherent in the CAO design. While it is possible to utilize the TOA scale as a self-assessment, we have moved away from it in favor of the following process. After showing a YouTube video that explains the TOA concept in general (https://www.youtube.com/watch?v=pkRSTZ4uWa4), ask students to reflect and score themselves on a scale of 1 (low) to 10 (high). Next, present a set of slides that describe a person with high TOA and a person with low TOA. Ask students to reflect on their self-assessment of their own TOA and adjust it if necessary. Next, ask students to stand in a line from lowest to highest TOA. While they are standing in this line, lead a discussion to explore the concept of TOA. Start with people on the low end and ask them to describe themselves in terms of TOA (how they deal with ambiguity, how it makes them feel, etc.). Then move to middle, then high.

To conclude this discussion, have the students count off into groups and discuss the following questions: (1) How do you think tolerance of ambiguity will help you in this class? (2) Do you think you need to grow in this area? If so, why? How do you plan to do that? (3) When you start a new job, how do you think your tolerance of ambiguity will affect your performance? Why? Give examples. If there is time, you can ask students to continue this discussion in the teams. Ask them to reflect on how the collective TOA in the team will contribute to and/or detract from effectively carrying out their responsibilities.

Homework

The homework this week consists of a number of Appreciative Inquiry exercises outlined in a separate packet (see Appendix 8). These exercises are designed to introduce students to positive organizational attitudes and behaviors. Briefly explain the concept of Appreciative Inquiry: how it works and why it's a powerful tool that is being leveraged in this course. Briefly walk them through the packet as there are parts that they need to do individually before their team meeting and parts that they need to do together (these are also described in the posted homework assignment). Remind them that you will lead class next week (week three), but after that you will be turning the class over to them.

Week 2: Team Homework (to be completed before class in week three)

In your group time this week you will complete the Appreciative Inquiry team packet. You can download it from Google Drive (URL or hyperlink) or you can choose to make a copy and save it to your own Google Drive.

• Part 1 – Individual Discovery

- Part 3 – Individual Vision

Your team will need to arrange a time to meet to complete the group elements (you will need about 1.5–2 hours):

- Part 2 – Team Discovery
- Part 4 – Team Vision
- Part 5 – Team Contract

By the time you finish the packet you will be ready to present your results in class next week. The packet will explain what you need to present in the next class. Your group answers will be posted here: (link to a Google doc where all teams post their answers).

Reading: Chapter 3 (quiz next week)

References

Budner, S. (1962), 'Intolerance of ambiguity as a personality variable', *Journal of Personality*, **30** (1), 29–50.
Neck, C. P., J. D. Houghton and E. L. Murray (2018), *Organizational Behavior: A Skill-Building Approach*, Los Angeles, CA: Sage Publications.

Appendix 8: Appreciative Inquiry team packet

ORGANIZATIONAL BEHAVIOR

Appreciative Inquiry for Team Formation:
Building a Foundation for High Performance

An Exceptional Classroom Organization:
Students as Leaders – Innovative Action – Transformational Learning

This packet contains the activities that will help you establish the foundation for high performance in your team. As with every aspect of this class, we will learn by doing.

We will assume your team already has the seeds of high performance within it. We will develop an understanding of this potential by sharing your stories about peak moments of success in our past team experiences. Normally, these narratives are invisible to us because they are taken for granted and do not demand our attention. By exploring past experiences of high performance you will develop an understanding of what you are doing when you are at your best. This awareness will serve as a resource, a reserve of energy and action.

Next, we will build a vision for the future of OB Inc. We will discuss how to translate this vision into reality. We will establish priorities, action groups, and real learning projects.

As we go through these discussions, pay close attention to the way you relate to one another. Listen carefully. Ask questions. Be respectful and interested in what others say.

Finally, these discussions should nurture the essential conditions of high performance: (1) **connectedness**, (2) **feedback**, and (3) and a capacity for **self-organizing**.

PART 1: INDIVIDUAL DISCOVERY

Overview

To establish a foundation for success in this organization, we will start by examining past, positive experiences of work in a team. In particular, we will explore what it means to be **an exceptional classroom organization** where **students are leaders**, engaged in **innovative action** to generate **transformational learning**.

Individually – Before you meet with your team, think through and take notes on the following topics:

Topic #1: Describe a Peak Experience in a Team

Think back to one particularly successful moment in your experience as a participant in a team or an organization. What happened, and who was involved?

What did this moment represent as a milestone of development or accomplishment for the people who took part? What was it about the experience that made it particularly meaningful to you, personally?

Topic #2: Explore your Strengths and Enabling Factors

Based on your story, what do you consider to be your strengths as a team member? (What might past teammates say are your greatest qualities?) Name at least three.

1. _____
2. _____
3. _____

PART 2: TEAM DISCOVERY – AN APPRECIATIVE CONVERSATION

Overview

This activity will help your team gather ideas, analyze them, and process some of the key themes in your collective experience.

Discuss Peak Stories and Strengths or Capabilities

1. Appoint a scribe and a time-keeper.
2. Go around the group and share your thoughts about topic #1. As you share, look for common themes in the peak stories. Make notes on the flipchart (or Google doc) as you go.
3. Go around the group and share your thoughts about topic #2 (strengths). As you share, look for common themes in the common or complementary strengths that unite your team. Make notes on the flipchart (or Google doc) as you go.
4. Choose a story to share from the group.
5. Based on what you have learned in this conversation, what do you consider to be your team's strengths? Which of these will contribute to your ability to become a high-performance team?
6. Appoint a spokesperson to present your team's work to the class, specifically the responses to #4 and #5 above.

PART 3: INDIVIDUAL VISION

Overview

During this class, our goal is to create a culture that supports the development of high performance, which will lead us to be **an exceptional classroom organization** where **students are leaders**, engaged in **innovative action** to generate **transformational learning**. Building on what you have learned in your earlier discussion, we will now imagine an ideal future for your team and this class.

Individually – Before you meet with your team, think through and take notes on the following topics:

1.   Explore a Vision for the Future of this Class and your Team

Imagine that it is 3–5 years from now. As you reflect back, this class and your team are seen as very significant parts of your education.

• What will you remember about the class and your team? What made it one of the best learning experiences you've ever had?

- What will have happened during the semester that will have made it a profound experience? What will be the outcome?
- As you look ahead, what would you like to see happen in the future of this class? Specifically:
  - How should class activities be managed? By whom?
  - What should the role of the professor be?
  - How should we evaluate the contributions of each team member?
  - How will you know that your group has become a high-performing team?

2.   Enabling Actions

If the above vision is to be actualized:

- What one action would bring us closer to your vision of the ideal future for your team and for this class?
- What are you, personally, willing to do to make it happen?
- What will be required of each member of your team and of this class if this vision is to be fulfilled?

PART 4: TEAM VISION

Overview

This activity will help us refine a vision of this class as we move from design to implementation.

Dialogue Instructions

1. Appoint a scribe. This person should capture a summary of your conversation and the ideas that emerge.
2. Go around the circle and ask each person to share answers to topic #1. The scribe should write down a few key words for each person.
3. Go around the circle and have each person share answers to topic #2. Again, write down key words for each person.
4. Review what the scribe has captured to identify common themes.

Prepare a Presentation

5. On a flipchart (or Google doc), write three key ideas or themes that define your team's vision for the future of this class.
6. Write the key commitments or actions needed from each member or team to make this vision happen.
7. Develop a creative presentation to illustrate your vision of the future – a skit, a poem, a rap, a game show, or other artistic rendition. Prepare to perform this presentation for the class.

PART 5: TEAM CONTRACT

Overview

This activity will help you become specific about your expectations for your team for the remainder of this class.

Dialogue/Development of a Team Contract

1. *Vision*: Discuss your vision for your team. Together, decide on the key themes that should indicate when your team is functioning at a high level of performance. Write a short **vision statement**. Then write "indicators" that will establish when your vision is in place.
2. *Norms*: Discuss norms that emerged from the "creative presenta-
   · tions." Select 3–5 norms that you would like to promote in your team as a condition for high performance. Write these norms as **expectations** in your team contract.
3. *Accountability*: Discuss how you will provide feedback to one another. How will you tell others that they are succeeding? How will you deal with moments when you are not contributing? Write several **accountability** statements to capture your expectations.
4. Select one person to write up the team contract and send it to the Performance Team for evaluation.

Appendix 9: Detailed instructions for week three

The first 7.5–9 hours of the course constitute the first phase of the CAO. This first phase is educator intensive; you will be in charge of the class for this first phase, and will turn responsibility over to the students for the next two phases. The purpose of the first phase of your CAO is to establish the ground rules of the organization as well as help students prepare for this course format and their upcoming responsibilities.

WEEK 3 (2.5–3 HOURS)

Before Class

Engage students who come to class early in arranging the class into a circle. Ultimately, they will decide how to configure the classroom to suit their needs. In these first weeks starting in a circle is meant to demonstrate that we will make the space work for us, and not vice versa.

The focus this week is to have the teams engage in appreciative inquiry, to set a positive tone for their work together, as well as preparation for taking over responsibility for the class next week.

Icebreaker Activity

Start class with a student-led get-to-know you activity or two depending on time available. These are the students who volunteered in week two to lead an activity. The purpose of this activity is to model full engagement, an active start to the session, and students taking responsibility. The norm of educator dependence is being challenged.

Individual and Group Quiz

This week you will administer an individual and group quiz on Chapter 3 (Neck, Houghton, & Murray, 2018), their reading assignment from last week. This follows the same process as outlined in Appendix 7 for week two.

Appreciative Inquiry Activity

Students completed the Appreciative Inquiry team packet (see Appendix 8) in their newly formed teams as homework, and are coming to class prepared with that information. This is an important process to facilitate as it contributes to the initial forming stage of team development (Tuckman, 1965).

Start by refreshing their memory of what AI is and why it is important for this course. The AI activity covers three topics: discover (peak team experiences and strengths), dream (vision for the future), and design (create a group contract). Start with discover, allowing each group to go around the room and share their thoughts (they wrote these down in a Google doc while doing their homework). Allow the other teams to ask any questions they may have of the presenting team. After all teams have shared, ask each team to describe their vision for the class and do their "special presentation." Before starting the "special presentations" remind the Culture and Coordination Team that they are going to use some of the material produced here to create class culture and rituals.

Team contracts are the last part of the AI packet deliverables. You may have teams share them or assign each team to review the contract of another team and give them suggestions on how to make it better (while also gathering ideas to improve their own contract).

Team Time for Getting Organized

Week three ends with "team time" for the students to plan how they will begin and maintain a functioning class starting in week four. Students may decide to work in teams for a while or start a larger class discussion to make some of the major decisions that need to be addressed before taking over the class next week. As you transition to the role of senior manager, your silence at this time, and at the beginning of week four, is critical. You want to allow a vacuum to develop that encourages the students to step forward and fill the silence. During this time you are available to answer questions that teams may have about their roles and responsibilities. It is critical to adopt a coaching stance at this point, not giving them definitive answers about how to perform their roles but rather asking them questions that will help them realize the opportunities that exist and lead them to make their own decisions. It's less important that they "do it right" and more important that they become fully involved in the process, taking initiative and experimenting by taking action. Mistakes and missteps will drive learning, so the focus is on thoughtful action rather than getting it right the first time.

During the process of planning for week four pay special attention to the Culture and Coordination Team since responsibility will fall on them to establish a class schedule and facilitate the class through the beginning stages of self-organizing. They will have questions for you, and you want to approach them with a supportive, coaching attitude rather than telling them what to do and how to do it.

There is also one team that will be teaching next week's content. Make sure that you make an appointment to meet with them before they leave class, and pose questions to them to be sure they are prepared for what is coming: How long will presentations be? Where will they find an activity? Do we need PowerPoint slides? What is the rubric for evaluating the presentation?, etc. Some of these questions can only be answered by other teams. For example, the rubric is the responsibility of the Feedback Team and so this question should be directed to them.

Homework

From now on you will not assign homework to the teams. Sometimes teams in class will assign team homework to the whole class, but otherwise the teams need to be self-directed about their team meeting time to be successful in the course.

> **Week 3 Team Homework**
>
> You are running an organization now. Decide how best to use your team time to complete organizational responsibilities. Remember that your goal is to become a high-functioning team, so focusing on team relationships and dynamics as well as getting tasks done is important.

References

Neck, C. P., J. D. Houghton and E. L. Murray (2018), *Organizational Behavior: A Skill-Building Approach*, Los Angeles, CA: Sage Publications.

Tuckman, B. W. (1965), 'Developmental sequence in small groups', *Psychological Bulletin*, **63** (6), 384–399.

References

Abeysekera, L. and P. Dawson (2015), 'Motivation and cognitive load in the flipped classroom: Definition, rationale and a call for research', *Higher Education Research & Development*, **34** (1), 1–14.

Albert, M. and B.J. Beatty (2014), 'Flipping the classroom applications to curriculum redesign for an introduction to management course: Impact on grades', *Journal of Education for Business*, **89** (8), 419–424.

Amundsen, S. and Ø.L. Martinsen, (2014), 'Empowering leadership: Construct clarification, conceptualization, and validation of a new scale', *Leadership Quarterly*, **25** (3), 487–511.

Anderson, L.W. and D.R. Krathwohl (eds) (2000), *A Taxonomy for Learning, Teaching, and Assessing: A Revision of Bloom's Taxonomy of Educational Objectives*, New York: Longman.

André, R. (2011), 'Using leadered groups in organizational behavior and management survey courses', *Journal of Management Education*, **35** (5), 596–619.

Ashenafi, M.M. (2017), 'Peer-assessment in higher education: Twenty-first century practices, challenges and the way forward', *Assessment & Evaluation in Higher Education*, **42** (2), 226–251.

Association to Advance Collegiate Schools of Business (2020), *2020 Standards for AACSB Business Accreditation*. Retrieved from: https://www.aacsb.edu/-/media/aacsb/docs/accreditation/business/standards-and-tables/2020%20aacsb%20business%20accreditation%20standards%20%20exposure%20draft%20no%201%20distributefinal.ashx?la=en&hash=E9B979E1F216730D3ABA637AA61CDEA29E7BB8CA.

Baeten, M., F. Dochy, and K. Struyven (2008), 'Students' approaches to learning and assessment preferences in a portfolio-based learning environment', *Instructional Science*, **36**, 359–374.

Balke, W.M. (1981), 'The policy learning co-op: Treating the classroom as an organization', *Organizational Behavior Teaching Journal*, **6** (2), 27–33.

Barry, D. (1990), 'Twincorp: Extensions of the classroom-as-organization model', *Organizational Behavior Teaching Review*, **14** (1), 1–15.

Bennis, W.G. and J. O'Toole (2005), 'How business schools lost their way', *Harvard Business Review*, **83** (5), 96–104.

Bergmann, J. and A. Sams (2012), *Flip Your Classroom: Reach Every Student in Every Class Every Day*, Washington, DC: International Society for Technology in Education.

Blood, M.R. (1994), 'The role of organizational behavior in the business school curriculum', in J. Greenberg (ed.), *Organizational Behavior: The State of the Science*, Hillsdale, NJ: Lawrence Erlbaum Associates, pp. 207–220.

Bloom, B.S., M.D. Engelhart, E.J. Furst, W.H. Hill, and D.R. Krathwohl (1956), *Taxonomy of Educational Objectives: The Classification of Educational Objectives. Handbook I: The Cognitive Domain*, White Plains, NY: Longman.

Boud, D. (2001), 'Making the move to peer learning', in D. Boud, R. Cohen, and J. Sampson (eds) (2001), *Peer Learning in Higher Education: Learning from and with Each Other*, London: Kogan Page, pp. 1–20.

Boud, D., R. Cohen, and J. Sampson (eds) (2014), *Peer Learning in Higher Education: Learning from and with Each Other*, Abingdon, UK: Routledge.

Bradford, D.L. (1975), 'Editorial comment', *Teaching of Organization Behavior*, **1** (1), 2.

Bradford, D.L. and A.R. Cohen (1981), 'Responding to student challenges', *Organizational Behavior Teaching Journal*, **6** (2), 20–26.

Bradford, D.L. and R. LeDuc (1975), 'One approach to the care and teaching of introductory organizational behavior', *Teaching of Organization Behavior*, **1** (1), 18–24.

Bradford, D.L. and J.I. Porras (1975), 'Restructuring the classroom: A design for a 36-person T-group', *Teaching of Organizational Behavior*, **1** (2), 16–19.

Brame, C. (2013), 'Flipping the classroom', Vanderbilt University Center for Teaching. Retrieved 29 July 2019 from http://cft.vanderbilt.edu/guides-sub-pages/flipping-the-classroom/.

Bransford, J.D., A.L. Brown, and R.R. Cocking (2000), *How People Learn: Brain, Mind, Experience, and School*, Washington DC: National Academy Press.

Bright, D.S. (2020), 'ProHealth or HealthCore: Teaching students about reality-creation in organizational life', *Management Teaching Review*, **5** (1), 59–69.

Bright, D.S. and E.F. Turesky (2010), 'Fostering student-to-student feedback: A condition for emergent learning in the classroom', paper presented at the Organizational Behavior Teaching Conference, Albuquerque, New Mexico.

Bright, D.S., A. Caza, E.F. Turesky, R. Putzel, E. Nelson, and R. Luechtefeld (2016), 'Constructivist meta-practices: When students design activities, lead others, and assess peers', *Journal of Leadership Education*, **15** (4), 75–99.

Bright, D.S., E.F. Turesky, R. Putzel, and T. Stang (2012), 'Professor as facilitator: Shaping an emerging, living system of shared leadership in the classroom', *Journal of Leadership Education*, **11** (1), 158–176.

Brown, R. and G. Murti (2003), 'Student partners in instruction: Third level student participation in advanced business courses', *Journal of Education for Business*, **79** (2), 85–89.

Budner, S. (1962), 'Intolerance of ambiguity as a personality variable', *Journal of Personality*, **30** (1), 29–50.

Bye, D., D. Pushkar, and M. Conway (2007), 'Motivation, interest, and positive affect in traditional and nontraditional undergraduate students', *Adult Education Quarterly*, **57** (2), 141–158.

Cameron, K. S., R.E. Quinn, J. DeGraff, and A.V. Thakor (2014), *Competing Values Leadership*, Cheltenham, UK and Northampton, MA, USA: Edward Elgar Publishing.

Carberry, A.R. and M.W. Ohland (2012), 'A review of learning-by-teaching for engineering educators', *Advances in Engineering Education*, **3** (2), 1–17.

Chappell, S. and D. Thomas (2019), 'The shadow side of teaching classroom-as-organization (CAO)', *Journal of Management Education*, **43** (4), 461–470.

Cheit, E.F. (1985), 'Business schools and their critics', *California Management Review*, **27** (3), 43–62.

Chrispeels, H.E., J.M. Chapman, C.L. Gibson, and G.K. Muday (2019), 'Peer teaching increases knowledge and changes perceptions about genetically modified crops in non-science major undergraduates', *CBE: Life Sciences Education*, **18** (2), art. 14.

Clare, D.A. (1976), 'Organizational Behavior, Inc.: Variation on a theme', *Teaching of Organizational Behavior*, **2** (3), 15–20.

Cohen, A.R. (1976), 'Beyond simulation: Treating the classroom as an organization', *Teaching of Organizational Behavior*, **2** (1), 13–19.

Cohen, A.R. (2019), Phone interview with D. Bright, S. Chappell, and D. Thomas.

Conger, J. A. and R.N. Kanungo (1988), 'The empowerment process: Integrating theory and practice', *Academy of Management Review*, **13** (3), 471–482.

Conklin, T.A. (2013), 'Making it personal: The importance of student experience in creating autonomy-supportive classrooms for millennial learners', *Journal of Management Education*, **37** (4), 499–538.

Cotton, C.C. (1975), 'When is reality not enough? The realism paradox in the simulation of a hierarchical organization', *Teaching of Organizational Behavior*, **1** (4), 25–28.

David, F.R. and F.R. David (2011), 'Comparing management curricula with management practice', *SAM Advanced Management Journal*, **76** (3), 48–55.

Dewey, J. (1938), *Experience and Education*, New York: Collier.

Dickinson, A.M. (2000), 'The historical roots of organizational behavior management in the private sector: The 1950s–1980s', *Journal of Organizational Behavior Management*, **20** (3–4), 9–58.

Dinsmore, D.L. and P.A. Alexander (2012), 'A critical discussion of deep and surface processing: What it means, how it is measured, the role of context, and model specification', *Educational Psychology Review*, **24** (4), 499–567.

Donovan, P. (2017), 'A threshold concept in managing: What students in introductory management courses must know', *Journal of Management Education*, **41** (6), 835–851.

Estes, C.A. (2004), 'Promoting student-centered learning in experiential education', *Journal of Experiential Education*, **27** (2), 141–160.

Falchikov, N. and J. Goldfinch (2000), 'Student peer assessment in higher education: A meta-analysis comparing peer and teacher marks', *Review of Educational Research*, **70** (3), 287–322.

Farashahi, M. and M. Tajeddin (2018), 'Effectiveness of teaching methods in business education: A comparison study on the learning outcomes of lectures, case studies and simulations', *International Journal of Management Education*, **16** (1), 131–142.

Finan, M.C. (1992), 'Manager and staff: A business communication course goes live!', *Journal of Management Education*, **16** (4), 479–493.

Fiorella, L. and R.E. Mayer (2013), 'The relative benefits of learning by teaching and teaching expectancy', *Contemporary Educational Psychology*, **38** (4), 281–288.

Fiorella, L. and R.E. Mayer (2016), 'Eight ways to promote generative learning', *Educational Psychology Review*, **28** (4), 717–741.

Fischer, F., I. Kollar, K. Stegmann, and C. Wecker (2013), 'Toward a script theory of guidance in computer-supported collaborative learning', *Educational Psychologist*, **48** (1), 56–66.

French, R. and P. Simpson (1999), 'Our best work happens when we don't know what we're doing', *Socio-Analysis*, **1** (2), 216–230.

Gardner, W.L. and L.L. Larson (1988), 'Practicing management in the classroom: Experience is the best teacher', *Organizational Behavior Teaching Review*, **12** (3), 12–23.

Ghoshal, S. (2005), 'Bad management theories are destroying good management practices', *Academy of Management Learning and Education*, **4** (1), 75–91.

Gielen, M. and B. De Wever (2015), 'Structuring peer assessment: Comparing the impact of the degree of structure on peer feedback content', *Computers in Human Behavior*, **52**, 315–325.

Goldschmid, B. and M.L. Goldschmid (1976), 'Peer teaching in higher education: A review', *Higher Education*, **5** (1), 9–33.

Goltz, S.M. (1992), 'Practicing management in the classroom', *Journal of Management Education*, **16** (4), 444–460.

Goodman, P.S. and D.A. Whetten (1998), 'Fifty years of organizational behavior from multiple perspectives', in J. McKelvey and M. Neufeld (eds), *Industrial Relations at the Dawn of the New Millennium*, Ithaca: New York State School of Industrial and Labor Relations, pp. 32–53.

Goodrick, E. (2002), 'From management as a vocation to management as a scientific activity: An institutional account of a paradigm shift', *Journal of Management*, **28** (5), 649–668.

Gordon, R.A. and J.E. Howell (1959), *Higher Education for Business*, New York: Columbia University Press.

Graf, L.A. and P.D. Couch (1984), 'A program for managing student groups: An applied organizational behavior experience', *Organizational Behavior Teaching Review*, **9** (4), 34–40.

Gruys, M.L. and D.S. Bright (2011), 'A service-oriented approach to teaching human resource management', *Journal of Human Resources Education*, **5** (1), 13–31.

Hake, R.R. (1998), 'Interactive-engagement vs. traditional methods: A six-thousand-student survey of mechanics test data for introductory physics courses', *American Journal of Physics*, **66** (1), 64–74.

Hannah, D.R. and R. Venkatachary (2010), 'Putting "organizations" into an organization theory course: A hybrid CAO model for teaching organization theory', *Journal of Management Education*, **34** (2), 200–223.

Hendry, J.R., T.B. Hiller, E.C. Martin, and N.M. Boyd (2017), 'Context and pedagogy: A quarter-century of change in an introductory management course', *Journal of Management Education*, **41** (3), 346–384.

Herrington, J. and R. Oliver (2000), 'An instructional design framework for authentic learning environments', *Educational Technology Research and Development*, **48** (3), 23–48.

Herrington, T. and J. Herrington (2005), 'What is an authentic learning environment?', in A. Herrington and J. Herrington (eds), *Authentic Learning Environments in Higher Education*, Hershey, PA: Information Science Publishing, pp. 1–13.

Highhouse, S. (2002), 'A history of the T-group and its early applications in management development', *Group Dynamics: Theory, Research, and Practice*, **6** (4), 277–290.

Houghton, J.D. and C.P. Neck (2002), 'The revised self-leadership questionnaire: Testing a hierarchical factor structure for self-leadership', *Journal of Managerial Psychology*, **17** (8), 672–691.

Hung, W., J.H. Bailey, and D.H. Jonassen (2003), 'Exploring the tensions of problem-based learning: Insights from research', *New Directions for Teaching and Learning*, **95**, 13–23.

Ingols, C. and M. Shapiro (2014), 'Concrete steps for assessing the "soft skills" in an MBA program', *Journal of Management Education*, **38** (3), 412–435.

Jones, M., C. Baldi, C. Phillips, and A. Waikar (2017), 'The hard truth about soft skills: What recruiters look for in business graduates', *College Student Journal*, **50** (3), 422–428.

Josefowitz, N. (1978), 'Assessment centers in the classroom', *Organizational Behavior Teaching Journal*, **3** (2), 27–29.

Kast, F.E. (1965), 'Management education in Europe', *Academy of Management Journal*, **8** (2), 75–89.

King, A. (2002), 'Structuring peer interaction to promote high-level cognitive processing', *Theory Into Practice*, **41** (1), 33–39.

Knight, J.K. and W.B. Wood (2005), 'Teaching more by lecturing less', *Cell Biology Education*, **4** (4), 298–310.

Knowles, M.S. (1980), *The Modern Practice of Adult Education*, New York: The Adult Education Company.

Koh, A.W.L., S.C. Lee, and S.W.H. Lim (2018), 'The learning benefits of teaching: A retrieval practice hypothesis', *Applied Cognitive Psychology*, **32** (3), 401–410.

Kolb, A.Y. and D.A. Kolb (2009), 'Experiential learning theory: A dynamic, holistic approach to management learning, education and development', in S.J. Armstrong and C.V. Fukami (eds), *The SAGE Handbook of Management Learning, Education and Development*, Los Angeles, CA: Sage Publications, pp. 42–68.

Kolb, D.A. (1984), *Experiential Learning: Experience as the Source of Learning and Development*, Englewood Cliffs, NJ: Prentice-Hall.

Kollar, I. and F. Fischer (2010), 'Peer assessment as collaborative learning: A cognitive perspective', *Learning and Instruction*, **20** (4), 344–348.

Könings, K.D., M. van Zundert, and J.J. van Merriënboer (2019), 'Scaffolding peer-assessment skills: Risk of interference with learning domain-specific skills?', *Learning and Instruction*, **60**, 85–94.

Kosnik, R.D., J.K. Tingle, and E.L. Blanton (2013), 'Transformational learning in business education: The pivotal role of experiential learning projects', *American Journal of Business Education*, **6** (6), 613.

Lawrence, A.T. (1992), 'Teaching high-commitment management the high-commitment way', *Journal of Management Education*, **16** (2), 163–180.

Leigh, E. (2003). *A Practitioner Researcher Perspective on Facilitating an Open, Infinite, Chaordic Simulation: Learning to Engage in Theory while Putting Myself into Practice* (Doctoral dissertation), University of Technology, Sydney, Australia.

Leigh, E. and L. Spindler (2004), 'Simulations and games as chaordic learning contexts', *Simulation & Gaming*, **35** (1), 53–69.

Leigh, E. and L. Spindler (2005), 'Congruent facilitation of simulations and games', in R. Shiratori, K. Arai, and F. Kato (eds), *Gaming, Simulations, and Society*, Tokyo, Japan: Springer, pp. 189–198.

Lencioni, P.M. (2012), *The Five Dysfunctions of a Team: Team Assessment*, San Francisco, CA: Wiley & Sons.

Lo, C.K., H.F. Hew, and G. Chen (2017), 'Toward a set of design principles for mathematics flipped classrooms: A synthesis of research in mathematics education', *Educational Research Review*, **22**, 50–73.

London, M.B. and B. Van Buskirk (2018), 'The co-created classroom: From teacher/student to mentor/apprentice', in J. Neal (ed.), *Handbook of Personal and Organizational Transformation*, New York: Springer, pp. 1051–1080.

Lynn, M.L. (2010), 'Venture Out: An entrepreneurial introduction to business', *Christian Business Academy Review*, **5**, 31–36.

Magoon, A. J. (1977), 'Constructivist approaches in educational research', *Review of Educational Research*, **47** (4), 651–693.

Mannion, R., S. Harrison, R. Jacobs, F. Konteh, K. Walshe, and H.T. Davies (2009), 'From cultural cohesion to rules and competition: The trajectory of senior management culture in English NHS hospitals, 2001–2008', *Journal of the Royal Society of Medicine*, **102** (8), 332–336.

Marton, F., and R. Säljö (1976), 'On qualitative differences in learning: Outcome as a function of learners' conception of task', *British Journal of Educational Psychology*, **46** (2), 115–127.

Mason, G., T. Shuman, and K. Cook (2013), 'Comparing the effectiveness of an inverted classroom to a traditional classroom in an upper-division engineering course', *IEEE Transactions on Education*, **56** (4), 430–435.

McDonald, M., K. Spence, and B. Sheehan (2011), 'Classroom-as-organization: An Integral approach', *Journal of Integral Theory & Practice*, **6** (2), 67–81.

McKeachie, W.J. (1990), 'Research on college teaching: The historical background', *Journal of Educational Psychology*, **82** (2), 189.

Meyer, G.W. and M.J. Gent (1998), 'Organization-as-classroom approaches to management education', in R.G. Milter, J.E. Stinson, and W.H. Gijslaers (eds), *Educational Innovation in Economics and Business III*, Dordrecht, Netherlands: Springer, pp. 99–113.

Mezoff, R.M., A.R. Cohen, and D.L. Bradford (1979), 'A dialogue on treating the classroom as an organization', *Organizational Behavior Teaching Journal*, **4** (1), 25–36.

Michaelsen, L.K., A.B. Knight, and L.D. Fink (2004), *Team-Based Learning: A Transformative Use of Small Groups in College Teaching*, London: Praeger.

Michinov, N., J. Morice, and V. Ferrières (2015), 'A step further in peer instruction: Using the stepladder technique to improve learning', *Computers & Education*, **91**, 1–13.

Miles, R.H. and W.A. Randolph (1979a), *The Organization Game*, Glenview, IL: Scott Foresman.

Miles, R.H. and W.A. Randolph (1979b), 'The organization game: A behaviorally played simulation', *Exchange: The Organizational Behavior Teaching Journal*, **4** (2), 31–34.

Miles, R.H. and W.A. Randolph (1984), *The Organization Game* (2nd ed.), Glenview, IL: Scott Foresman.

Miller, J.A. (1991), 'Experiencing management: A comprehensive, "hands-on" model for the introductory undergraduate management course', *Journal of Management Education*, **15** (2), 151–169.

Miller, J.A. (2017), 'Lessons from Management 101: Learning to manage ourselves', *Journal of Management Education*, **41** (3), 335–345.

Mishler, E. (1979), 'Meaning in context: Is there any other kind?', *Harvard Educational Review*, **49** (1), pp. 1–19.

Missildine, K., R. Fountain, L. Summers, and K. Gosselin, (2013), 'Flipping the classroom to improve student performance and satisfaction', *Journal of Nursing Education*, **52** (10), 597–599.

Morgan, G. (1986), *Images of Organization*, Newbury Park, CA: Sage Publications.

Nath, R. (1975), 'The management training laboratory: An experiential orientation to the MBA program', *Teaching of Organizational Behavior*, **1** (2), 10–15.

National Association of Colleges and Employers (2018), 'Employers want to see these attributes on students' resumes'. Retrieved 19 October 2019 from https://www.naceweb.org/talent-acquisition/candidate-selection/employers-want-to-see-these-attributes-on-students-resumes/.

Neck, C.P., J.D. Houghton, and E.L. Murray (2018), *Organizational Behavior: A Skill-Building Approach*, Los Angeles, CA: Sage Publications.

O'Brien, C.D.A. and A.F. Buono (1996), 'Creating a networked, learning organization in the classroom', *Journal of Management Education*, **20** (3), 369–381.

Obert, S.L. (1982), 'Teaching micro OD skills by developing the classroom organization', *Organizational Behavior Teaching Journal*, **7** (1), 23–26.

Oddou, G.R. (1987), 'Managing organizational realities: A classroom simulation', *Organizational Behavior Teaching Review*, **11** (3), 72–85.

Okita, S.Y., S. Turkay, M. Kim, and Y. Murai (2013), 'Learning by teaching with virtual peers and the effects of technological design choices on learning', *Computers & Education*, **63**, 176–196.

Organisation for Economic Co-operation and Development (2017), 'Future of work and skills', paper presented at the 2nd Meeting of the G20 Employment Working Group, Hamburg, Germany, 17–20 March.

Pendse, S. (1984), '*E pluribus unum*: Making a classroom an organization', *Organizational Behavior Teaching Review*, **9** (4), 41–51.

Peng, X., D. Zhang, M. Jackson, B. Yalvac, A, Ketsetzi, D. Eseryel, and T.F. Eyupoglu (2019), 'Examining the learning by teaching method in computer-aided design instruction', *Computer-Aided Design and Application*, **16** (1), 129–139.

Pfeiffer, J.W. and J.E. Jones (1974), 'Group on group: A feedback experience', in J.W. Pfeiffer and J.E. Jones (eds), *A Handbook of Structured Experiences for Human Relations Training* (vol. 1, rev. ed.), San Diego, CA: University Associates.

Pfeffer, J. and C.T. Fong (2002), 'The end of business schools? Less success than meets the eye', *Academy of Management Learning and Education*, **1** (1), 78–95.

Pierson, F.C. (1959), *The Education of American Businessmen: A Study of University-College Programs in Business Administration*, New York: McGraw-Hill.

Poirier, T.I. (2017), 'Is lecturing obsolete? Advocating for high value transformative lecturing', *American Journal of Pharmaceutical Education*, **81** (5), 83.

Putzel, R. (1992), 'Experience base learning: A classroom-as-organization using delegated, rank-order grading', *Journal of Management Education*, **16** (2), 204–219.

Putzel, R. (2006), 'Drawing on peer evaluation studies to manage the classroom', *Journal of Business & Leadership: Research, Practice, and Teaching (2005–2012)*, **2** (2), art. 13.

Putzel, R. (2007), 'XB: New paradigm management of the classroom as a complex organization. *Journal of Business & Leadership: Research, Practice, and Teaching*, **3** (1), 136–143.

Putzel, R. (2013), *XB Manual for a Learning Organization (Version 3.5)*, Colchester, VT: Roger Putzel Publishing.

Raab, N. (1997), 'Becoming an expert in not knowing: Reframing educator as consultant', *Management Learning*, **28** (2), 161–175.

Ramsey, V.J. and D.E. Fitzgibbons (2005), 'Being in the classroom', *Journal of Management Education*, **29** (2), 333–356.

Randolph, W.A. and Miles, R H. (1979), 'The organization game: A behaviorally played simulation', *Organizational Behavior Teaching Journal*, **4** (2), 31–35.

Readwritethink.com (n.d.), Retrieved from http://www.readwritethink.org/.

Ritter, B.A., E.E. Small, J.W. Mortimer, and J.L. Doll (2018), 'Designing management curriculum for workplace readiness: Developing students' soft skills', *Journal of Management Education*, **42** (1), 80–103.

Romme, A.G.L. (2003), 'Organizing education by drawing on organization studies', *Organization Studies*, **24** (5), 697–720.

Romme, A.G.L. and R. Putzel (2003), 'Designing management education: Practice what you teach', *Simulation & Gaming*, **34** (4), 512–530.

Roscoe, R.D. (2014), 'Self-monitoring and knowledge-building in learning by teaching', *Instructional Science*, **42**, 327–351.

Ryan, R. and E. Deci (2000), 'Self-determination theory and the facilitation of intrinsic motivation, social development, and well-being', *American Psychologist*, **55** (1), 68–78.

Schermerhorn, J.R., Jr., J.G. Hunt, and R.N. Osborn (1982), *Instructor's Manual to Accompany Managing Organizational Behavior* (2nd ed.), New York: Wiley.

Schneier, C.E. (1975), 'Resolving the content issue in the introductory OB course: Using a problem-centered approach', *Teaching of Organizational Behavior*, **1** (3), 12–18.

Scott, C.D. and D.T. Jaffe (1988), 'Survive and thrive in times of change', *Training & Development Journal*, **42** (4), 25–28.

Sheehan, B.J., M.A. McDonald, and K.K. Spence (2009), 'Developing students' emotional competency using the classroom-as-organization approach', *Journal of Management Education*, **33** (1), 77–98.

Slavin, R.E. (1983), *Cooperative Learning*, New York: Longman.

Sleeth, R.G. and D.R. Brown (1984), 'Plan the intensity of your exercises', *Organizational Behavior Teaching Review*, **9** (2), 60–71.

Smith, T.W. and S.A. Colby (2007), 'Teaching for deep learning', *The Clearing House: A Journal of Educational Strategies, Issues and Ideas*, **80** (5), 205–210.

Spooren, P., B. Brockx, and D. Mortelmans (2013), 'On the validity of student evaluation of teaching: The state of the art', *Review of Educational Research*, **83** (4), 598–642.

Spreitzer, G.M. (1995), 'Individual empowerment in the workplace: Dimensions, measurement, and validation', *Academy of Management Journal*, **38** (5), 1442–1465.

Steenberg, V.V. and J.H. Gillette (1984), 'Teaching group dynamics with a group-on-group design', *Exchange: The Organizational Behavior Teaching Journal*, **9** (2), 14–29.

Strayer, J.F. (2012), 'How learning in an inverted classroom influences cooperation, innovation and task orientation', *Learning Environments Research*, **15** (2), 171–193.

Strijbos, J.W. and D. Sluijsmans (2010), 'Unravelling peer assessment: Methodological, functional, and conceptual developments', *Learning and Instruction*, **20**, 265–269.

Sun, J.C.Y. and Y.T. Wu (2016), 'Analysis of learning achievement and teacher–student interactions in flipped and conventional classrooms', *International Review of Research in Open and Distributed Learning*, **17** (1), 79–99.

Taber, K.S. (2006), 'Beyond constructivism: The progressive research programme into learning science', *Studies in Science Education*, **42** (1), 125–184.

Tan, C., W.G. Yue, and Y. Fu (2017), 'Effectiveness of flipped classrooms in nursing education: Systematic review and meta-analysis', *Chinese Nursing Research*, **4** (4), 192–200.

Thomas, K.W. and B.A. Velthouse (1990), 'Cognitive elements of empowerment: An "interpretive" model of intrinsic task motivation', *Academy of Management Review*, **15** (4), 666–681.

Topping, K.J. (1996), 'The effectiveness of peer tutoring in further and higher education: A typology and review of the literature', *Higher Education*, **32** (3), 321–345.

Topping, K.J. (1998), 'Peer assessment between students in colleges and universities', *Review of Educational Research*, **68** (3), 249–276.

Topping, K.J. (2005), 'Trends in peer learning', *Educational Psychology*, **25**, 631–645.

Topping, K.J. (2009), 'Peer assessment', *Theory Into Practice*, **48** (1), 20–27.

Tubbs, S.L. (1985), 'Consulting teams: A methodology for teaching integrated management skills', *Exchange: The Organizational Behavior Teaching Journal*, **9** (4), 52–57.

Tuckman, B.W. (1965), 'Developmental sequence in small groups', *Psychological Bulletin*, **63** (6), 384–399.

Tuckman, B.W. and M.A.C. Jensen (1977), 'Stages of small-group development revisited', *Group & Organization Studies*, **2** (4), 419–427.

Tyson, T. and L. Taylor (2000), 'Excitement and anxiety in the first-year experiential classroom', in *Proceedings of 4th Pacific Rim Conference of First Year in Higher Education*, Brisbane, Australia: Queensland University of Technology.

Ültanır, E. (2012), 'An epistemological glance at the constructivist approach: Constructivist learning in Dewey, Piaget, and Montessori', *International Journal of Instruction*, **5** (2), 195–212.

Uttl, B., C.A. White, and D.W. Gonzalez (2017), 'Meta-analysis of faculty's teaching effectiveness: Student evaluation of teaching ratings and student learning are not related', *Studies in Educational Evaluation*, **54**, 22–42.

van Alten, D.C., C. Phielix, J. Janssen, and L. Kester (2019), 'Effects of flipping the classroom on learning outcomes and satisfaction: A meta-analysis', *Educational Research Review*, **28**, 1–18.

van Baarle, S., S.A. Dolmans, A.S. Bobelyn, and A.G.L. Romme (2019), 'Beyond command and control: Tensions arising from empowerment initiatives', *Organization Studies*, https://doi.org/10.1177/0170840618818600 (online first pp. 1–23).

van Seggelen-Damen, I.C. and A.G.L. Romme (2014), 'Reflective questioning in management education: Lessons from supervising thesis projects', *SAGE Open*, **4** (2), https://doi.org/10.1177/2158244014539167.

van Zundert, M., D. Sluijsmans, and J. van Merriënboer (2010), 'Effective peer assessment processes: Research findings and future directions', *Learning and Instruction*, **20** (4), 270–279.

Webster, R.S. (2015), 'In defence of the lecture', *Australian Journal of Teacher Education*, **40** (10), 88–105.

Weil, J.L. (1988), 'Management experientially taught', *Organizational Behavior Teaching Review*, **12** (3), 54–61.

Weil, S.W. and I. McGill (1989), *Making Sense of Experiential Learning: Diversity in Theory and Practice*. Milton Keynes, UK: Open University Press.

Weimer, M. (2013), *Learner-Centered Teaching: Five Key Changes to Practice*. Hoboken, NJ: Wiley & Sons.

Worren, N. (2018), *Organization Design: Simplifying Complex Systems*. London: Routledge.

Yakubovich, V. and R. Burg (2019), 'Friendship by assignment? From formal interdependence to informal relations in organizations', *Human Relations*, **72** (6), 1013–1038.

Yu, Z. and G. Wang (2016), 'Academic achievements and satisfaction of the clicker-aided flipped business English writing class', *Educational Technology & Society*, **19** (2), 298–312.

Zainuddin, Z. and M. Attaran (2016), 'Malaysian students' perceptions of flipped classroom: A case study', *Innovations in Education and Teaching International*, **53** (6), 660–670.

Zhou, X., L.H. Chen, and C.L. Chen (2019), 'Collaborative learning by teaching: A pedagogy between learner-centered and learner-driven', *Sustainability*, **11** (4), 1–14.

Index